MANJU'S
COOKBOOK

**VEGETARIAN
GUJARATI INDIAN
RECIPES FROM A
MUCH-LOVED FAMILY
RESTAURANT**

MANJU PATEL

PHOTOGRAPHY BY CLARE WINFIELD

RYLAND PETERS & SMALL
LONDON • NEW YORK

**In loving memory
of my dear husband
(Shirish Patel)**

Senior designer Megan Smith
Senior editor Abi Waters
Creative director Leslie Harrington
Editorial director Julia Charles
Production manager Gordana Simakovic
Manju's team of chefs Manju Patel,
   Dipali Patel and Kirti Patel
Food stylist Troy Willis
Props stylist Hannah Wilkinson
Indexer Vanessa Bird
Illustrator Lyndon Hayes

First published in 2023 by
Ryland Peters & Small
20–21 Jockey's Fields,
London WC1R 4BW
and 341 E 116th Street
New York NY 10029

www.rylandpeters.com

Text © Manju Patel 2023
Design and commissioned photographs
© Ryland Peters & Small 2023

ISBN: 978-1-78879-559-3

10 9 8 7 6 5 4 3 2 1

Printed and bound in China

A CIP record for this book is available
from the British Library. CIP data from the
Library of Congress has been applied for.

NOTES

• Both British (metric) and American (imperial
or US cups) are included; however, it's important
not to alternate between the two within a recipe.
• All spoon measurements are level unless specified
otherwise.
• Ovens should be preheated to the specified
temperatures. If using a fan-assisted oven, adjust
according to the manufacturer's instructions.
• When a recipe calls for the grated zest of citrus
fruit, buy unwaxed fruit and wash well before using.
If you can only find treated fruit, scrub well in warm
soapy water before using.
• Always use a wide, deep pan when deep-frying
food and use an oil with a high smoke point. Use
a thermometer to check that the oil is hot enough
for deep-frying (180°C/350°F).
• Each recipe is labelled with the following icons
where relevant:

(V) Vegan (GF) Gluten Free (NF) Nut Free

When using asafoetida, some brands use gluten
in the manufacturing process. We always use a
gluten-free variety, but please check your chosen
brand before using.

CONTENTS

INTRODUCTION

They say 'home is where the heart is'. Although my heart is now most definitely in Brighton, a seaside city on the south coast of England, I am forever Gujarati. At home, we eat Gujarati food as though we were back in India.

My father moved to Kenya to seek his fortune as Africa was a land of hope. He settled in Kenya and worked in a port in Mombassa. My mother was a housewife and after a few years they moved to Kampala in Uganda and opened a grocery store.

It was customary for expectant mothers to go back to her parents to have the baby. So when my mother became pregnant with me, she returned to India. The journey involved taking a train to Mombassa and a boat journey to India, which lasted many weeks.

Then she took another train to Gujarat where I was born in 1936. After a few months, my mother and I returned to Kampala to be with my father.

Like most young daughters, I helped my mother to cook for the family from a very early age. Uganda is a lush, fertile land where crops grow abundantly, so we used to cook whatever was in season. My mother stuck to her Gujarati heritage and cooked in the same way. We ate a lot of green vegetables and curries such as *Giloda Bateta nu Shaak* (Ivy Gourd and Potato Curry, see page 51) and *mogu nu shaak* (cassava curry). Gujarati cuisine places vegetables first and enhances flavours by balancing spices.

By now I had a younger brother and sister and my eldest sister was married and went to live with her husband. Then at the age of 12, tragedy struck. My father passed away suddenly. My sister was 7 and my younger brother was only 4. My mother, a very strong-willed and determined woman, was left to raise three very young children. She had an intense work ethic and she was a special cook. Mum started a tiffin business, supplying home-cooked meals to other Asians who were all missing the food they enjoyed back in India.

I didn't go to school as mother and I were making around 35 tiffins every morning, ready for collection. They would be filled with two curries – one vegetable, such as potato and aubergine/eggplant and a dal such as moong dal. We would also include bread, rice, *papad* (poppadoms), pickles and *mithai* (Indian sweets). My love for cooking grew from this early age: selecting vegetables at markets, grinding spices and making blends as a child beside my mother. The smells, aromas and smiling faces when people enjoyed our food enhanced my passion. At the age of 14, I was able to cook all the tiffins by myself and my mother could branch out to tutor local kids from our neighbourhood. It was hard, but it meant we were able to send my siblings to good schools to gain an education.

I met my husband, Shirish, and shortly afterward we were married. I left home and went to live with his large family. His mother was a very strict Jain, a religion similar to Hinduism but with severe dietary restrictions. Meat, fish and eggs are completely forbidden as well as root vegetables, which host many micro-organisms that die when they are uprooted. I had to totally change my cooking style and adapt to the dietary requirements of my new family. There are also set times when food can be consumed according to Jainism, which added another aspect that I needed to consider.

My husband started a coffee storage business (Uganda was one of the major coffee producers at the time). His business flourished and he branched out into coffee production, owning two factories just outside of Kampala, the capital of Uganda. In 1965, my eldest son Jaymin was born and our second son Naimesh arrived in 1970. Life was very comfortable, but I was still responsible for cooking for the entire family.

In 1972, the president of Uganda, Idi Amin, decided to expel all Asians from the country giving them just 90 days' notice to leave. He was a brutal dictator who then went on to kill any Asians left behind.

Our choice was simple, either we return to India or we go to the UK. We had British passports so we decided to go there. Alongside tens of thousands of Asians, we left everything behind in Uganda, including our homes, businesses and friends and family who went to other countries instead. Everything was so very different – the country, language, customs and culture. Also, it was freezing cold!

We were allowed to take our clothes from Uganda, but in the chaos at Heathrow, some of our suitcases went missing, never to return. My younger brother had arrived in the UK a few years earlier so he organized for us to rent a couple of rooms with another Indian family near Alexandra Palace in London.

Just days after arriving, I found a job as a factory worker with MK Electricals, a large company making electrical plugs and sockets. London in the 1970s was full of factories and jobs were easy to come by. It wasn't glamorous, but it was secure. Shirish also took a job in a factory making car lamps. A few days after arriving in the UK, our house was burgled and the few clothes and possessions we did have were vandalized and ruined.

Slowly we rebuilt our lives, but throughout all of this upheaval, our recipes stayed the same. Some ingredients that we were used to cooking with in Uganda were hard to come in the UK, and the smell of cooking with garlic would annoy the neighbours. How things have changed? Large family gatherings were common and we made festivals, such as Diwali, special by cooking Indian sweets and snacks. My brother would continuously push me towards opening a food catering business or restaurant. However, money was tight and the risks were too great. I had the passion for cooking and dreamed of owning my own business, but at that point I didn't feel I could take the risk.

As my boys grew into adults, they ended up in Brighton running a gift store. My family is everything to me, so when grandchildren started to arrive, Shirish and I moved to Brighton to be with them. I had retired after 30 years of operating a machine and packing boxes and was now free.

On a sunny afternoon in April 2017, my sons drove me to a small street in North Laines, Brighton. As we pulled up, I noticed a board above a commercial premises that had 'Manju's' written on it. As we entered, I noticed something unusual – some of my belongings were hung on the walls and my cooking utensils were on display. Then it hit me – they had bought me a restaurant! I was 80 years old at the time and FINALLY I had my own restaurant. I cry easily, but there were many tears of happiness that day.

Manju's opened on 16th April 2017 serving vegetarian Gujarati food. Our food is mostly unrecognizable from the dishes served in curry houses. Real Indian food is not widely available, but things are getting better. At Manju's, we are determined that the restaurant uses the same cooking principles and techniques taught to me by my mother – a love for fresh vegetables and spices combined in dishes that bring happiness.

I am so lucky that my youngest son is married to Dee, a chef who has worked in restaurants for many years, and along with my other daughter-in-law Kirti, we run Manju's kitchen together. My two sons are front of house and, at weekends, my grandchildren work in the restaurant. Although, I'm sure like other teenagers, they'd rather be spending time with their friends instead!

Manju's has gained a fantastic reputation that we are incredibly proud of. We receive a lot of love and support from our local community. Our job is to champion real Indian food, in particular vegetarian Gujarati food, and change the common perception of Indian food.

Welcome to *Manju's Cookbook*. We hope you enjoy cooking and experimenting with our recipes. Most of all we hope it brings you happiness through our food.

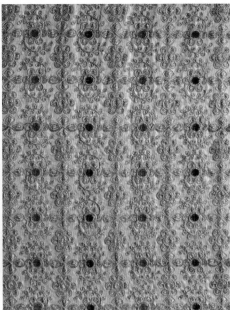

MANJU'S

Our wonderful family-run restaurant in the heart of Brighton is loved by so many and is a true reflection of the Gujarati way of cooking. It is also where we produce our delicious range of chutneys.

GUJARATI CUISINE

For many, 'eating Indian' conjures up images of restaurants decorated with flocked wallpaper that serve up chicken tikka (not even a real Indian dish) and machismo-challenging vindaloo, all washed down with cold beers. This is simply not accurate! Real Indian food cooked by Indian people is a symphony of delicate tastes, textures and fragrances based on home-cooked recipes handed down over generations.

Gujarat is a state on the west coast of India, north of Mumbai. Religion, geography and custom play a huge part in the food of the region, but the influence of Hinduism and Jainism means the cuisine is vegetable led. About 2,000 years ago all three major Indian religions – Hinduism, Jainism and Buddhism – championed non-violence as an ethical value and food consumed as a result of animal slaughter was widely considered as a form of violence against life forms, so it became a

religious and socially unacceptable way to eat. Jainism respects all life forms and avoids food produced in a way that harms any living creature.

The climate also has a large influence on Gujarati food. The temperature in Gujarat varies from very mild winters to scorching hot summers when the temperature can shoot up to 50°C/104°F so salt, lemon and sugar is added to the food to prevent dehydration. The weather impacts which crops can grow as vegetables that require a moderate climate struggle. The crops that are grown in quantity are potatoes, onions, garlic, okra and tomatoes, to name just a few.

The food varies regionally and even according to the tastes of each individual family. Gujarati food has been part of my daily diet my whole life and every Sunday we have a large family meal consisting of a couple of curries, dal, rice and lots of sides. We don't have starters, mains and desserts, but large pans are placed in the middle of the table for everybody to help themselves. The idea is to balance the meal with hot, sweet and sour tastes. A Gujarati *thali* is the best example of this. It consists of a couple of curries – one with sauce and one dry – bread to scoop up the curry like a spoon, rice, a dal, a fiery pickle and a sweet to balance the heat.

We love to snack, and have containers filled with goodies, such as Gathiya (see page 115), ready to open whenever we fancy. When we have visitors, a big pot of Masala Chai (see page 164) is a must to accompany snacks. Gujarati's naturally have a sweet tooth – Sheero (see page 159) and Lapsi (see page 155) are eaten during festivals and on happy occasions such as weddings and birthdays.

Indian cooking is not an exact science. Adapt these recipes to suit your tastes and go with the flow, but most of all, have fun!

THE GUJARATI PANTRY

SPICES

ASAFOETIDA *(hing)* A pungent powder used to flavour oils in small quantities. Store in an airtight container.

CARDAMOM *(elachi)* Available in various forms and as a powder, but green cardamom in pods is most widely used. Has a strong distinct flavour.

CAROM SEEDS *(ajmo)* These tiny seeds are strong in flavour, so a little goes a long way. They are used to temper oils and have herbal properties so are sometimes used to treat digestive issues.

RED CHILLI/CHILE POWDER *(lal mirchu)* There are so many varieties of chilli, all varying in strength so adjust accordingly. Kashmiri chilli powder is less fiery and adds a wonderful colour to dishes.

CINNAMON *(taj)* Widely used to add a warm nutty flavour to main dishes, desserts and rice.

CLOVES *(larving)* A strong spice often used whole in cooking. A powdered form is used in spice blends, such as Masala Chai (see page 164).

CORIANDER *(dhania)* One of the most common spices in our cooking. Found whole or in powdered forms, it's best to use whole seeds and then crush them just before using.

CUMIN *(jeeru)* These can be whole or ground and often used alongside ground coriander. If using cumin seeds it is best to crush them before use.

CURRY LEAVES *(limri)* Use fresh leaves, if you can find them. Usually added to oil to make a vagar (hot tempered oil).

FENUGREEK *(methi)* These are available fresh, seeded or crushed. They are bitter in taste and widely used in Indian cooking.

GARAM MASALA A spice blend used in many dishes and can easily be bought. Most common spices included are cinnamon, cardamom, cumin, black pepper and cloves.

MUSTARD SEEDS *(rai)* There are different types, but our recipes mainly use brown mustard seeds.

TURMERIC *(haldi)* This is available fresh or in powdered form. Our dishes use ground turmeric, which is one of the most popular spices in Indian cooking. A strong yellow powder, use only a little as it can overpower a dish if too much is added.

STORECUPBOARD STAPLES

BASMATI RICE There are so many varieties of rice, but basmati is the one we use. It is generally considered the best type for Indian cooking as it is long-grained and has a lovely fragrance.

CHICKPEA/GRAM FLOUR *(besan)* This flour is made from grinding chana dal and is widely used to make a batter for bhajia (fritters) and also in some Indian sweets.

CHANA DAL *(yellow split peas)* Used to make one of the most common dals. They require soaking before use.

MOONG DAL *(yellow split mung beans)* These don't require soaking and are easy to digest so can be consumed by babies.

SEV Crispy chickpea noodles that are used in street-food dishes or eaten as a snack (see page 111).

TUVAR DAL *(yellow lentils/dried pigeon peas)* This dal needs more preparation than most as it needs to be washed properly and requires a longer soaking time.

URAD DAL *(split black gram)* These lentils, used in Dahi Vada (see page 130) are from the same family as moong dal, but do require soaking before using.

MOST-USED VEGETABLES

Gujarat is a very fertile land. Most people who live in the villages work in agriculture. The climate affects which crops can grow and vegetables are usually consumed seasonally. Even though you can get hold of most vegetables all year round now, we would always recommend using seasonal produce where possible. Here are a few Indian vegetables that you may not be familiar with and that we love to use in our cooking.

BHINDA *(okra/lady fingers)* You either love or hate this vegetable as some people find them too slimy. When cooked properly though, okra hold spices really well so work perfectly in our dishes.

DHUDHI *(bottle gourd)* Part of the gourd family, this vegetable has a lovely soft texture which works well with chana dal or in Handvo (see page 19).

GHILODA *(tindora/ivy gourd)* This gourd is also known as baby watermelon due to its appearance. It can be used in a curry on its own or with other vegetables. Look out for the slim ones when shopping.

GUVAR *(cluster beans)* These beans are long and narrow with a pointed end, which are normally topped and tailed before cooking. They are slightly bitter in taste. If you cannot find guvar, use green beans instead.

VALOR BEANS *(hyacinth beans)* This is a very common bean in Gujarat. Every part of the plant is edible and can be used. It is a flat green bean with a smooth skin. If you cannot find valor beans, use runner beans instead.

SPICE PASTES

If you cook a lot of Indian dishes, having these essential pastes ready-made and to hand can be a time saver. Home-made pastes are far better than shop-bought ones; they are fresh with no added preservatives and are so simple to make. It's fair to say Indian cooking often requires a lot of ingredients and time, so whatever you can prepare ahead is a real bonus.

GINGER & CHILLI PASTE

10 green chillies/chiles
8–10-cm/3¼–4-in. piece of fresh ginger, peeled
pinch of salt

MAKES ABOUT 60 G/¼ CUP

GINGER, GARLIC & CHILLI PASTE

12–13 garlic cloves, peeled
5–6-cm/2–2½-in. piece of fresh ginger, peeled
20 green chillies/chiles
pinch of salt

MAKES ABOUT 150 G/⅔ CUP

GINGER & GARLIC PASTE

12–13 garlic cloves, peeled
5–6-cm/2–2½-in. piece of fresh ginger, peeled
1 teaspoon sunflower oil

MAKES ABOUT 100 G/SCANT ½ CUP

Place all the ingredients in a food processor or blender and blitz to a smooth paste. Add a little water (or oil for the Ginger and Garlic Paste) if needed to loosen. These pastes can be stored in an airtight container in the fridge for 3–4 days. Just add to curries as required.

FARSAN
SHARING

DHOKLA
SAVOURY STEAMED SPONGE CAKE
(V) (GF) (NF)

There is nothing more Gujarati than dhokla! As the dhokla batter is steamed, before being tempered with spiced oil and curry leaves, use a steamer if you have one, otherwise just follow the steps shown here. Serve as a breakfast or snack with Lili Chutney (see page 147).

1½ teaspoons salt
⅛ teaspoon ground turmeric
2 tablespoons icing/
  confectioners' sugar
2½ tablespoons sunflower oil
1½ tablespoons Ginger and Chilli
  Paste (see page 14)
2 tablespoons fresh lemon juice
300 g/2¼ cups chickpea/gram
  flour
1 tablespoon Eno fruit salts
  (see Note below)
pinch of red chilli/chile powder

VAGAR (TEMPERED OIL)
60 ml/¼ cup sunflower oil
½ tablespoon mustard seeds
½ tablespoon sesame seeds
½ teaspoon asafoetida
10 curry leaves
2 tablespoons icing/
  confectioners' sugar

TO SERVE
fresh coriander/cilantro
grated fresh coconut
Lili Chutney (see page 147)

*23 cm/9 in round cake pan, at
least 7 cm/3 in deep, greased*

SERVES 4

Pour 400 ml/1¾ cups water into a bowl and add the salt, turmeric, icing sugar and oil. Use a balloon whisk to mix together until the sugar has dissolved. Add the ginger and chilli paste and lemon juice and mix well.

Sift the chickpea flour into a separate bowl.

Slowly start to add the wet mixture to the chickpea flour, stirring gently to combine. Once it has all been added, whisk quickly to make a batter that is not too thick and not too runny.

To create the steamer, place a large deep saucepan on the hob/stove top. Fill a smaller pan with no handles with water so that it is filled nearly to the top, then place this inside the large deep pan. This will ensure the smaller pan doesn't move around while the dhokla are steaming.

Fill the deep pan with enough water so it reaches nearly to the top of the smaller pan, leaving a gap of about 1 cm/½ in. Place over a high heat, cover with a lid and bring the water to the boil.

Give the batter a quick stir and then add the Eno fruit salt to the batter. Whisk quickly for 30 seconds; the batter will change colour and become thicker.

Transfer the batter to the greased cake pan and lightly sprinkle red chilli powder on top.

Place the cake pan inside the steamer resting on top of the smaller pan and place a lid on top. Wrap a clean dish towel around the edges to ensure steam doesn't escape. Steam for 18–20 minutes. Check if the dhokla are ready by inserting a knife into the middle; if it comes out clean, they are ready, otherwise steam for a little longer and check again.

Once the dhokla are nearly ready, make the vagar. Heat the oil in a small pan over a high heat. Once the oil is ready, add the mustard seeds. When the seeds start to crackle, add the rest of the ingredients as well as 120 ml/½ cup water and cook for 5 minutes, stirring occasionally.

When the dhokla are ready, remove from the steamer and pour the vagar over the top. Garnish with coriander and sprinkle grated coconut over the top. Cut into squares and serve with Lili Chutney.

NOTE *The Eno fruit salts in this recipe can be bought from pharmacies. They have a similar effect to baking powder and are used as a leavening agent.*

HANDVO
LENTIL CAKE TOPPED WITH SESAME SEEDS
(V) (NF)

Handvo is made by grinding rice and lentils together to make a batter, which is then filled with vegetables and tempered spices. The batter mix can be bought ready-made in Asian grocery shops, but nothing beats the home-made kind. Various vegetables can be added to handvo; in this recipe I have used bottle gourd and carrots, although courgettes/zucchini also work well. I really love the golden crust provided by the sesame seeds.

DOUGH
500 g/2¾ cups basmati rice
200 g/1 cup tuvar dal (yellow lentils/dried pigeon peas)
50 g/¼ cup chana dal (split skinned black chickpeas)
400 g/14 oz. dhudhi (bottle gourd), peeled and grated/shredded
1 small carrot, grated/shredded
100 g/¾ cup chapati atta (wholemeal/whole-wheat flour)
80 ml/⅓ cup sunflower oil, plus extra for greasing
½ teaspoon bicarbonate of soda (baking soda)

MASALA MIX
1 tablespoon salt
3 tablespoons granulated sugar
pinch of ground turmeric
3 tablespoons Ginger, Garlic and Chilli Paste (see page 14)
2 tablespoons fresh lemon juice

VAGAR (TEMPERED OIL)
80 ml/⅓ cup sunflower oil
1 tablespoon mustard seeds
1 tablespoon sesame seeds
½ teaspoon fenugreek seeds
½ teaspoon asafoetida

GARNISH
sesame seeds
red chilli/chile powder

30 x 25 cm/12 x 10 in baking sheet, at least 4 cm/1½ in deep, greased

SERVES 4

Place the rice, tuvar and chana dal in a large bowl and wash several times until the water runs clear.

Add 240 ml/1 cup cold water so the rice and dal mixture is completely covered and leave to soak for at least 2–3 hours, but ideally overnight.

Preheat the oven to 160°C fan/ 180°C/350°F/Gas 4 and grease the prepared baking sheet with oil, making sure the sides are well greased.

Drain the mixture, discard the water and transfer to a blender. Add 240 ml/1 cup fresh cold water and blend to a coarse paste, being careful to not overdo it.

Transfer to a large bowl, add the dhudhi and carrots and fold into the mixture. Add the chapati atta, oil and bicarbonate of soda and mix together well.

Make the masala mix in a separate bowl. Place the salt, sugar, turmeric, ginger, garlic and chilli paste and lemon juice in the bowl, mix well and then add to the rice-dal mixture. Combine well.

To make the vagar, heat the oil in a small pan over a medium heat for 1 minute. Add the mustard seeds and once they start to crackle, add the rest of the ingredients. Quickly swirl the pan and immediately pour the tempered oil into the rice-dal mixture. Mix well to combine.

Transfer the mixture to the greased baking sheet and gently shake to evenly spread the mixture across the tray.

Liberally scatter sesame seeds over the top of the mixture and then lightly dust with chilli powder.

Bake on the middle shelf of the preheated oven for about 80–90 minutes or until the handvo develops a lovely dark golden crust. Check if the handvo is ready by inserting a knife into the middle; if it comes out clean, it is ready. Remove from oven and leave to cool for 10–15 minutes.

Cut into squares before serving.

KHANDVI
SAVOURY GRAM FLOUR & YOGURT ROLLS
(GF) (NF)

Khandvi are a delicious, melt-in-your-mouth snack from Gujarat. These seasoned chickpea/gram flour and yogurt rolls are spicy and slightly sweet and sour. Make sure you work out any lumps in the batter, then once the batter is the right consistency, work quickly.

BATTER
160 g/⅔ cup plain yogurt
½ teaspoon salt
pinch of ground turmeric
½ teaspoon Ginger and Garlic Paste (see page 14)
160 g/1¼ cups chickpea/gram flour

VAGAR (TEMPERED OIL)
2 tablespoons sunflower oil, plus extra for greasing
1 teaspoon mustard seeds
1 teaspoon sesame seeds
10 curry leaves
¼ teaspoon asafoetida

TO SERVE
2 tablespoons chopped fresh coriander/cilantro
2 tablespoons grated fresh coconut

SERVES 4

First, make the batter. Place all the ingredients in a bowl with 300 ml/1¼ cups cold water. Use a handheld blender to mix together until smooth, making sure there are no lumps.

Clean and very lightly grease a flat work surface.

Place the batter in a non-stick saucepan and cook over the lowest heat, stirring continuously with a silicon spatula to make sure the batter doesn't stick to the bottom of the pan. Once the batter starts to thicken, start to work more quickly, making sure no lumps form in the batter. Keep stirring until the batter sticks to the spatula.

To check if the batter is ready, spread a tiny piece onto the greased work surface and leave to cool for 2–3 minutes. If the batter sets and rolls easily, it's ready.

Now work very quickly! Spread the batter over the greased work surface and use a spatula or palette knife to spread it as evenly as possible. Spread all the batter as thinly as you can preferably about 2–3 mm/⅛ in. thick. Allow the batter to set.

Use the back of a knife to slice the khandvi into long strips about 4–5 cm/1½–2 in. wide and about 15–20 cm/6–8 in. long. Trim away any excess around the edges.

Use your fingers to slowly roll the khandvi tightly and place them on a plate.

To make the vagar, place the oil in a small saucepan over a high heat for 1 minute. Add the mustard seeds and once they start to crackle, add the rest of the ingredients. Quickly swirl around the pan a couple of times, then immediately pour the tempered oil over the khandvi.

Garnish with coriander and sprinkle grated fresh coconut over the top to serve. The khandvi can be stored in an airtight container in the fridge for up to 3 days.

KACHORI
SPICY PEAS WRAPPED IN PASTRY
(V) (NF)

When guests come to visit, I often serve these small spiced pastries as a snack before a main meal. It takes time to envelope each kachori in pastry, but go slowly and try to wrap each one evenly and without splitting the dough.

DOUGH
130 g/1 cup plain/all-purpose flour
¼ teaspoon salt
45 ml/3 tablespoons sunflower oil, plus extra for greasing and deep-frying

KACHORI
250 g/1⅔ cups fresh peas (defrosted if using frozen)
1 tablespoon sunflower oil
1 teaspoon mustard seeds
⅓ teaspoon asafoetida
20 g/¾ oz. semolina
1 teaspoon Ginger and Garlic Paste (see page 14)
1 teaspoon red chilli/chile powder
½ teaspoon salt
¾ teaspoon garam masala
1½ teaspoons fresh lemon juice
1 tablespoon granulated sugar

TO SERVE
Lili Chutney (see page 147) or Amli Chutney (see page 147)

MAKES 8

To make the dough, place the flour, salt and oil in a wide bowl and gently mix together. Slowly add 70 ml/⅓ cup cold water a little at a time and stir to combine. Add a few drops of oil to the palms of your hands and knead the dough until it is smooth and comes away cleanly from the bowl. Cover with a dish towel and leave the dough to rest for 15 minutes.

To make the kachori, place the peas in a blender or food processor and give them a quick blitz using the pulse setting, if you have one. The peas should be partially crushed but not fully blended into tiny pieces.

Heat the oil in a frying pan/skillet over a medium heat for 2–3 minutes. Check the oil is hot enough by placing a few mustard seeds in the pan; if they sizzle, the oil is ready. Reduce the heat to medium-low and then add the mustard seeds. Quickly stir and add the asafoetida and semolina. Keep stirring until the semolina becomes golden brown.

Add the crushed peas to the pan and stir gently to mix together. Cook for 3–4 minutes, stirring continuously. Add the rest of the ingredients to the pan, mix well and continue to cook, stirring continuously, for 3–4 minutes.

Remove the pan from the heat and spread the pea mixture out on a plate and leave to cool.

Once the pea mixture is cool enough to handle, roll it into 8 equal balls using a gentle pressure so the balls hold their shape.

Give the prepared dough a quick knead, then divide it into 8 pieces, rolling each into a ball.

Take a dough ball and gently stretch it into a palm-sized circle. Add a pea ball in the centre of the dough and carefully wrap the dough around it so that the peas are completely covered. Press the dough to seal the ball and remove any excess dough.

Gently roll and smooth each ball in between the palms of your hands and place on a plate. Repeat until everything has been used up.

Heat enough oil for deep-frying in a wide pan or wok over a high heat for 3 minutes. Check the oil is ready by placing a piece of dough into the oil; if the dough rises to the surface, the oil is ready.

Gently roll each dough ball in your hands before lowering into the hot oil. Deep-fry a few at a time but avoid them touching each other too much. Cook, turning occasionally, for 4–5 minutes until golden all over. Remove from the oil and place on kitchen paper. Repeat until all have been fried. Serve with chutney.

NOTE *You can freeze the kachori, just make sure you defrost them before deep-frying and serve them piping hot.*

BHINDA FRIES

OKRA FRIES

(V) (GF) (NF)

The okra in this lovely snack or starter are not slimy at all, which is something that normally puts people off using this vegetable. When okra fries are on the menu, they are always one of our bestsellers. My boys enjoy these fries and tell me they make great beer snacks, but I don't drink so will take their word for it!

100 g/3½ oz. okra, washed and dried
⅓ teaspoon salt
1 teaspoon red chilli/chile powder
⅛ teaspoon ground turmeric
¼ teaspoon ground coriander
½ teaspoon garam masala
½ teaspoon amchur powder (dried mango powder)
½ tablespoon Ginger and Garlic Paste (see page 14)
½ tablespoon chickpea/gram flour
¼ teaspoon rice flour
½ teaspoon cornflour/cornstarch
⅛ teaspoon fresh lemon juice
vegetable oil, for deep-frying
pinch of chaat masala

SERVES 2

Cut the tops off each okra, then slice them into thin fries. Place the okra in a large bowl and add the salt. Use your fingers to rub the salt into the okra so that the moisture starts to be released. Leave to rest for a couple of minutes.

Add the chilli powder, turmeric, ground coriander, garam masala, amchur powder and ginger and garlic paste to the okra. Mix well so that the okra are well covered.

Move the okra to one side of the bowl. Sift the chickpea flour and rice flour into the other side of the bowl. Add the cornflour and mix together thoroughly. Add the lemon juice and mix again.

Gradually incorporate the okra into the flour mixture and mix so that all the okra are well coated. Add a few drops of water to help bind the flour to the okra if needed.

Use your fingers to press the okra down into the flour, then transfer them to a sieve/fine-mesh strainer and shake to remove any excess flour.

Heat enough oil for deep-frying in a heavy-based pan or wok over a high heat for 2 minutes. To check if the oil is ready, add a piece of okra to the oil; if it sizzles, the oil is hot enough.

Lower the okra into the hot oil, making sure you don't overcrowd the pan. Cook, stirring occasionally, for 3–4 minutes or until the okra are golden brown.

Remove the okra fries from the oil and place on kitchen paper to drain. Sprinkle the chaat masala over the top and leave the okra to rest. The okra fries will become crispy once cooled.

Enjoy with a cold beer!

KERA NA BHAJIA

BANANA FRITTERS

(V) (GF) (NF)

Whenever I cooked these at home, my youngest son would gobble them down as soon as they were cool enough to eat. Later, he started to eat them with cinnamon sugar and chocolate as a dessert. This is most definitely not the traditional way of eating these bhajia! I like to use ripe bananas that have just started to develop a few brown spots on the skin as they have the most flavour. Definitely avoid using unripe bananas.

sunflower oil, for frying
2 ripe bananas, peeled and cut
    into 2–3 cm/1–1¼ in. pieces
    (or larger if preferred)
pea shoots, to garnish (optional)

BATTER
100 g/¾ cup chickpea/gram four
½ teaspoon salt
¼ teaspoon ground turmeric
½ teaspoon red chilli/chile
    powder
large pinch of bicarbonate of
    soda (baking soda)
½ teaspoon Ginger, Garlic and
    Chilli Paste (see page 14)
½ teaspoon fresh lemon juice

SERVES 2

To make the batter, sift the chickpea flour into a bowl. Add all the dry ingredients, mix well to combine and then add the ginger, paste and lemon juice. Add a drizzle of water and start mixing the wet ingredients into the flour. Gradually add about 120 ml/½ cup water, adding a little at a time and stirring until you have a batter the consistency of double/heavy cream.

Heat enough oil for deep-frying in a heavy-based pan or wok over a medium heat.

Add the bananas to the prepared batter and stir so that they are well coated.

Check the oil is hot enough for frying by adding a few drops of batter to the oil; if the batter rises, the oil is ready.

Take a banana piece out of the batter and gently shake to remove any excess batter. Lower the banana into the oil and repeat with a few more banana pieces, making sure they don't touch each other in the oil.

Fry for about 15–20 seconds and then carefully start to move them around in the oil. Turn over and fry the other side, moving them gently and making sure they don't touch each other in the oil.

Fry until golden all over, then remove the bhajia from the oil and place on kitchen paper to drain. Repeat with the remaining pieces of banana. Serve the bhajia straight away garnished with pea shoots if liked.

METHI NA GOTA
FENUGREEK LEAF FRITTERS
(V) (NF)

This popular snack on the streets of Gujarat is made by using fresh methi leaves (fenugreek). Although these leaves are quite bitter, they work wonderfully when balanced with spices. The centre of the fritters are soft and spongy once cooked, but once cooled they will become hard and so really are best served straight away.

2 tablespoons sunflower oil
50 g/1¾ oz. semolina
150 g/generous 1 cup chickpea/ gram flour
½ teaspoon black peppercorns
½ teaspoon coriander seeds
1 teaspoon carom seeds
¾ teaspoon salt
1 teaspoon granulated sugar
½ tablespoon Ginger and Garlic Paste (see page 14)
2 tablespoons fresh lemon juice
100 g/3½ oz. fresh fenugreek leaves, torn in half (these are bitter, so use less if preferred)
1 teaspoon baking powder
2 teaspoon Eno fruit salts (see Note opposite)
⅛ teaspoon ground turmeric
2 green chillies/chiles, finely chopped
vegetable oil, for deep-frying

TO SERVE
Lili Chutney (see page 147), Amli Chutney (see page 147) or Lal Chutney (see page 140)

MAKES ABOUT 35 FRITTERS

Place the sunflower oil in a pan over a high heat. Add the semolina and cook for 2 minutes, stirring continuously, until the semolina turns golden brown. Remove the pan from the heat and sift the chickpea flour into the semolina.

Crush the black peppercorns and coriander seeds in a pestle and mortar and add this to the pan.

Add the carom seeds, salt, sugar, ginger and garlic paste and stir to combine all the ingredients

Add the lemon juice, fenugreek leaves, baking powder, fruit salts, turmeric and chillies and mix until combined.

Add some water, a little at a time, and start to combine into a thick, lump-free batter.

Heat enough oil for deep-frying in a heavy-based pan or wok over a high heat. Once the oil is hot, reduce the heat to medium.

Wet your hands slightly and take about a tablespoon of batter, about the size of a golf ball, and lower it into the hot oil.

Repeat with more batter, adding a few more balls, making sure they don't touch each other in the oil. Fry for about 2 minutes before moving them gently. Turn and fry for about 5 minutes until the fritters are golden and crispy.

Remove the fritters from the oil and place on kitchen paper to drain.

Wet your hands again and repeat until all the fritters have been fried.

Serve hot with your choice of chutney on the side for dipping.

NOTE *Eno fruit salts are used in baking but are also a treatment for indigestion. They can be bought from pharmacies.*

BATETA NA BHAJIA
POTATO FRITTERS
(V) (GF) (NF)

My late husband was slightly obsessed with these bhajia and would wait patiently for the first batch to come off the stove. He'd beam as I laid a plate of bhajia and chutney before him. They are made by thinly slicing potatoes, coating them in a spicy chickpea flour batter and frying until crisp. This recipe will take your potatoes to the next level – just make sure you serve them immediately after frying. At the restaurant, we have used courgettes/ zucchini instead of potatoes in the past, which work just as well.

4 potatoes
sunflower oil, for deep-frying

BATTER
120 g/scant 1 cup chickpea/ gram flour
120 g/scant 1 cup cornflour/ cornstarch
120 g/scant 1 cup rice flour
1½ teaspoons salt
½ teaspoon ground turmeric
4 tablespoons Ginger, Garlic and Chilli Paste (see page 14)
juice of ½ lemon
large handful of chopped fresh coriander/cilantro

TO SERVE
Amli Chutney (see page 147) or Lal Chutney (see page 140)

SERVES 4

Sift the chickpea flour, cornflour and rice flour into a mixing bowl to remove any lumps. Add the salt, turmeric, ginger, garlic and chilli paste, lemon juice and chopped coriander and mix together.

Add about 80 ml/⅓ cup water, a little at a time, and keep mixing until the batter is smooth. You are looking for a consistency that is not too runny and not too thick.

Peel the potatoes and carefully slice them as thinly as possible – use a mandolin, if you have one, or otherwise use a sharp knife.

Place the potato slices in a sieve/strainer, rinse under cold running water and then dry on a clean dish towel.

Heat enough oil for deep-frying in a heavy-based pan or wok over a medium heat for 2–3 minutes. Check if the oil is hot enough by placing a few drops of the batter into the oil; if the batter rises, the oil is ready.

Drop a few slices of potato into the batter, coating them completely, and then shake off any excess batter.

Gently lower the battered potato slices into the hot oil and fry, turning over every so often, for a few minutes or until golden brown. Remove the bhajia from the oil and place on kitchen paper to drain any.

Serve hot with your choice of chutneys.

BATETA VADA
MASHED POTATO FRITTERS
(V) (GF) (NF)

Bateta Vada are hugely popular and eaten all over India. Spicy mashed potato is covered in batter, deep-fried until golden and served with chutney. These fritters make a great snack and are generally served hot, but also taste delicious eaten cold.

2 potatoes, boiled in their skins
1 teaspoon salt
20 g/4 teaspoons granulated sugar
1 teaspoon fresh lemon juice
handful of chopped fresh coriander/cilantro
1 teaspoon garam masala
20 g/¾ oz. Ginger, Garlic and Chilli Paste (see page 14)
2 teaspoons pomegranate seeds
2 teaspoons sultanas/golden raisins, roughly chopped
sunflower oil, for shaping and deep-frying
Amli Chutney (see page 147), to serve

BATTER
50 g/⅓ cup chickpea/gram flour
30 g/2 tablespoons cornflour/cornstarch
pinch of salt
¼ teaspoon fresh lemon juice

MAKES 12

To make the batter, sift the chickpea flour and cornflour into a bowl. Add the salt and lemon juice and slowly start to combine by gradually adding water, a little at a time – you should only need about 60 ml/¼ cup. Continue mixing until the batter is smooth and free of any lumps. The batter should not be too runny but thick enough to coat a spoon. Set aside.

Peel the boiled potatoes and grate into a bowl to a medium thickness. Add all the remaining ingredients, except the sunflower oil and chutney, to the potatoes and mix well, so everything is combined and the potato is mashed.

Add a few drops of oil to the palms of your hands, then slowly roll the potato mixture into 12 equal-sized balls and place on a plate.

Heat enough oil for deep-frying in a large frying pan/skillet over a high heat for 2 minutes. Check if the oil is hot enough by dropping a piece of batter into the oil; if the batter rises, the oil is ready.

Lower the heat to medium. Take a few potato balls and roll them in the batter, making sure the balls are completely coated. Shake off any excess batter and carefully lower the balls into the hot oil.

Using a slotted spoon, move the potato balls gently, turning them over every so often, making sure they don't stick together in the oil. Cook for 3–4 minutes or until golden brown. Remove the vada from the oil and place on kitchen paper to drain.

Continue cooking the vada in batches until all the potato balls are used up.

Serve either hot or cold with Amli Chutney.

KHANDA PALAK BHAJIA
SPINACH & ONION FRITTERS
(V) (GF) (NF)

These are an all-time classic! These crisp and tasty deep-fried spinach fritters are made with spinach leaves, chickpea/gram flour, onion and spices. Just make sure you cut the onions in the correct direction and cook the fritters gently otherwise they will be crispy on the outside yet uncooked inside.

2 white onions, peeled
¾ teaspoon salt
2 teaspoons red chilli/chile powder
¼ teaspoon ground turmeric
1 teaspoon garam masala
1 teaspoon carom seeds
100 g/3½ oz. chickpea/gram flour
large handful of fresh spinach, chopped
2 handfuls of chopped fresh coriander/cilantro
sunflower oil, for deep-frying
Lili Chutney (see page 147), to serve

MAKES 6

Cut the tops and bottoms from the onions and then slice each in half. Place each onion half flat side down, so the root and top are facing horizontally. Finely slice the onion vertically into thin half moons. Repeat until all the onions are sliced. Separate each slice of onion into individual layers and place in a wide bowl.

Add the salt, chilli powder, turmeric, garam masala and carom seeds to the onions and use your fingers to mix so that the onions are completely coated.

Sift the chickpea flour onto the onions and add the chopped spinach and coriander to the mix. Combine really well using your fingers, adding a few drops of water if needed to help bind the mixture together.

Place a heavy-based pan or wok over a low-medium heat and add enough oil for deep-frying.

Check if the oil is hot enough by placing a slice of onion into the pan; if it gently fries, the oil is ready. Now, don't wait to fry the onions, do it straight away!

Take a fistful of the onion mixture and carefully drop it into the oil to fry. Don't be tempted to shape or roll the mixture.

Repeat with a few handfuls of the onion mixture and increase the heat to high. Fry for 1 minute over a high heat, then turn the heat down to low. Gently fry, moving the bhajia in the oil and turning occasionally, for 2–3 minutes or until golden brown. Remove the bhajia from the oil and place on kitchen paper to drain. Repeat until all the bhajia are fried.

Serve hot with chutney and a cold beer!

SAMOSA
SPICED MIXED VEGETABLE SAMOSA

There is nothing better than homemade samosa! The beauty of making them yourself is that you can adjust the spices and vegetables to your taste.

60 ml/¼ cup sunflower oil,
    plus extra for deep-frying
1 teaspoon cumin seeds
1 teaspoon sesame seeds
⅓ teaspoon asafoetida
2 carrots, peeled and finely diced
4–5 white potatoes, peeled and
    finely diced
250 g/1⅔ cups fresh peas
    (defrosted if using frozen)
1 tablespoon fresh lemon juice

MASALA MIX
1 teaspoon salt
1 teaspoon red chilli/chile powder
1 teaspoon garam masala
½ teaspoon ground cinnamon
1 tablespoon granulated sugar
1 tablespoon Ginger, Garlic and
    Chilli Paste (see page 14)

PASTRY
125 g/scant 1 cup plain/
    all-purpose flour, plus extra
    for dusting
¼ teaspoon salt
¼ teaspoon fresh lemon juice

GLUE
2 tablespoons plain/all-purpose
    flour

TO SERVE
Amli Chutney (see page 147)
    or Lal Chutney (see page 140)
lemon wedges, for squeezing

MAKES ABOUT 34 SAMOSA

NOTE *If you are not vegan, these are delicious served with Masala Chai (see page 164)*

Heat the oil in a wide pan over a medium heat. Add the cumin and sesame seeds. Once they begin to crackle, add the asafoetida and carrots. Mix well, cover and cook for 2 minutes, stirring occasionally. Add the potatoes, cover and cook for 4–5 minutes. Add the peas, cover and cook for 2 minutes.

Add all the ingredients for the masala mix and combine, stirring gently. After 2 minutes, add the lemon juice and heat for 3–4 minutes. Remove the pan from the heat and spread the vegetables out on a plate to cool.

To make the pastry, sift the flour into a bowl and add the salt and lemon juice. Mix together, then slowly add 100 ml/scant ½ cup water, a little at a time. Knead the dough for 5 minutes until smooth but firm. Cover with a damp cloth and leave to rest for 15 minutes.

Place a frying pan/skillet over a low heat. Take a piece of dough, about 15 g/¾ oz. in weight, cover it in flour and roll into a 12 cm/5 in. circle. Place to one side. Repeat with another piece of dough so you have a second circle the same size.

Brush the second circle lightly with oil and dust in a little flour. Place the first circle on top and roll both together into a 15–16 cm/ 6–6½ in. circle.

Place the larger circle in the frying pan. Fry for 20 seconds, then flip over and fry on the other side. Try peeling back the top layer of pastry; once it comes away, take both layers off the heat and place on a plate, one on top of the other. Make sure not to overcook the pastry! Cover with a dish towel.

Repeat until all the dough has been rolled, very lightly fried and stacked. Use a sharp knife to cut the pastry circles into semi-circles.

For the glue, mix the flour with ¼ teaspoon water to a paste.

To shape the samosa, take a pastry semi-circle and fold one end of the straight edge two-thirds into the pastry. Use your finger to cover the other straight edge in glue and fold over to form a triangular pocket. Press the glued edge down to seal. Make sure the point created at the bottom of the triangle is completely closed and there is no hole.

Add a spoonful of the vegetables into the pocket. Use your finger to glue the top of the samosa and press to seal. Repeat until all the samosa are filled.

Heat enough oil for deep-frying in a heavy-based pan or wok over a medium heat for 3–4 minutes until the oil is very hot. Press the sides of each samosa again to make sure they are sealed, then lower them into the hot oil. Fry for 30 seconds, turn over and fry the other side. Repeat until both sides are golden brown. Remove the samosas from the oil and place on kitchen paper to drain. Repeat until all the samosa have been fried. Serve with chutney and lemon wedges for squeezing over.

PALAK BHAJIA
STUFFED SPINACH LEAF ROLLS
(V) (NF)

Patra is the traditional name given to this dish. Normally colocasia leaves would be used, but these can be very difficult to get hold of and so we have adapted this recipe to use large spinach leaves instead. Make sure you use the largest leaves you can find.

400 g/14 oz. fresh large leaf spinach (do not use baby leaf spinach)
grated fresh coconut, to garnish

BATTER
500 g/3¾ cups chickpea/gram flour
100 g/¾ cup chapati atta (wholemeal/whole-wheat flour)
1 teaspoon carom seeds
1 teaspoon ground turmeric
1 teaspoon red chilli/chile powder
2 tablespoons Ginger, Garlic and Chilli Paste (see page 14)
2 tablespoons sunflower oil
1½ tablespoons salt
2 tablespoons granulated sugar
½ tablespoon garam masala
⅛ teaspoon bicarbonate of soda (baking soda)
1 tablespoon fresh lemon juice

VAGAR (TEMPERED OIL)
2 tablespoons sunflower oil
1 tablespoon mustard seeds
2 garlic cloves, chopped
2 tablespoons sesame seeds

SERVES 4

Using a sharp knife, remove the veins from the spinach leaves but do not cut the leaves fully in half. Wash the leaves, drain and set aside to dry.

To make the batter, sift the chickpea flour into a large bowl and press through any lumps. Add all the remaining batter ingredients to the flour. Mix well and then slowly add 600 ml/2½ cups water, a little at a time. Using a balloon whisk, mix to make a smooth but thick batter. Make sure there are no lumps, then set aside for 10–15 minutes.

Place a heatproof bowl upside down in a large saucepan to make a steamer. Pour in enough water to nearly fill to the top, then place a lightly oiled plate on top. Make sure the water does not touch the plate. Place over a medium heat and bring the water to the boil.

On a clean work surface, place one of the largest spinach leaves upside down (vein side up) and pointed end away from you. Work using the largest leaves to the smallest leaves when battering. Generously cover the leaf with batter using a spatula or your hands, making sure it is completely coated. Place another leaf on top so it overlaps the first one, the pointed end away from you. Cover with batter again, then place another leaf on top, pointed end of the first leaf overlapping it. Cover with batter

and place another leaf at the tip of the second leaf. Place a couple of the smaller leaves in the middle and cover with batter.

Gently fold one side of the leaves towards the middle and then the other side towards the middle so you have straight sides and a rectangular shape. Add more batter to the folded sides and then start to roll the leaves tightly away from you. Take care and go slowly until you end up with a tightly rolled log shape. Repeat with the remaining leaves until all the bhajia have been rolled.

Place the spinach rolls on the oiled plate in the steamer and cover with a tight lid. Steam over a high heat for 20–25 minutes. Check if the bhajia are ready by carefully inserting a knife into one; if it comes away cleanly, they are ready.

Turn off the heat and remove the bhajia, leaving them to cool for 10 minutes. Once cooled. slice into small pinwheels.

Now, make the vagar. Heat the oil in a small frying pan/skillet over a high heat. Add the mustard seeds and once they stop crackling, add the garlic. Fry until the garlic is golden, then add the sesame seeds. Fry for a further 30 seconds, swirl the pan and then immediately pour the oil over the bhajia. Garnish with grated coconut and serve.

SHAAK
CURRIES

MATAR RINGAR NU SHAAK

PEA & AUBERGINE CURRY

(V) (GF) (NF)

Gujaratis love aubergine/eggplant and it is used a lot in our cooking. Unfortunately, aubergines are neglected in other cuisines as sometimes people find them a bit boring and too mushy. When cooked correctly, they have a wonderful texture that absorbs spices really well. This pea and aubergine curry is so easy to make. Use fresh peas, if you can, but frozen will work just as well at a push. As this curry doesn't have a sauce, I always serve this dish with Gujarati Dal (see page 103).

1 large aubergine/eggplant, chopped into 3-cm/1-in. cubes
140 ml/generous ½ cup sunflower oil
1 teaspoon mustard seeds
¼ teaspoon fenugreek seeds
⅓ teaspoon asafoetida
500 g/4 cups fresh or frozen peas (defrosted if frozen)
⅔ teaspoon ground turmeric
1 teaspoon red chilli/chile powder
2 teaspoons ground coriander
pinch of salt
⅓ teaspoon garam masala
chopped fresh coriander/cilantro, to garnish

TO SERVE
Rotli (see page 86) or your choice of rice dish (see pages 99–100)
Gujarati Dal (see page 103)

SERVES 4

Place the aubergine in a bowl of cold water to stop it browning.

Heat the oil in a large pan with a lid over a medium heat for 1 minute. Check if the oil is hot enough by adding a few mustard seeds to the oil; if the seeds crackle, the oil is ready, otherwise let the oil heat for a bit longer.

Once the oil is hot enough, add the mustard seeds and stir for 20 seconds. Add the fenugreek seeds and asafoetida, then stir quickly to combine. Drain and add the aubergine to the pan and stir to coat each piece in the spiced oil. Cover with the lid and leave to cook for 2 minutes. Give the aubergine a quick stir, cover again and cook for 5–6 minutes or until slightly tender and soft. Add the peas to the aubergine.

Add the turmeric, chilli powder, ground coriander, salt and garam masala and stir, coating the vegetables. Cover with the lid and leave to cook for 2 minutes.

Lift the lid, allowing any water from the lid to fall back into the pan. Stir again and cover. Once the aubergine is soft, tender and breaks apart easily, remove the pan from the heat. Transfer the curry to a serving bowl and garnish with chopped coriander.

Serve with rotli or rice and Gujarati Dal.

DHUDHI CHANA NU SHAAK
BOTTLE GOURD & CHANA DAL CURRY
(V) (GF) (NF)

This Gujarati curry is made with dhudhi (bottle gourd) and chana dal (also known as Bengal gram, split skinned black chickpeas or yellow split peas). I love the textures in this curry; the softness of the dhudhi works really well with the dal. When buying dhudhi, choose a bottle gourd with a smooth skin, that is pale green in colour and free from any blemishes. It should be firm and the flesh should not feel soft when pressed. Dhudhi can be found in most Asian grocery shops, but if you are really struggling to get hold of it, you can substitute with courgettes/zucchini instead.

400 g/2¼ cups chana dal
  (yellow split peas)
1 litre/4 cups boiling water, for
  soaking, plus another 800 ml/
  3½ cups for cooking the dal
1 large dhudhi (bottle gourd)
300 ml/1¼ cups sunflower oil
1 tablespoon cumin seeds
3 dried red chillies/chilis
5 cloves
1 cinnamon stick, about 4 cm/
  1½ in. long
¼ teaspoon asafoetida
250 ml/1 cup canned chopped
  tomatoes
1 teaspoon fresh lemon juice
chopped fresh coriander/cilantro,
  to garnish
Rotli (see page 86) and rice
  (see page 99), to serve

MASALA MIX
1 tablespoon Kashmiri chilli/chile
  powder
1½ teaspoons red chilli/chile
  powder
1 tablespoon ground coriander
1 teaspoon ground cumin
¼ teaspoon ground turmeric
1½ teaspoons salt
½ teaspoon garam masala
1 tablespoon granulated sugar
1 teaspoon Ginger, Garlic and
  Chilli Paste (see page 14)

SERVES 6

Place the chana dal in a large bowl, pour over the boiling water and leave to soak for 2 hours. Drain in a sieve/strainer and wash under cold running water several times. Drain again, return to the bowl and set aside.

Cut off the ends of the dhudhi and use a peeler to remove the outer green skin. Cut the dhudhi into 4-cm/1½-in. cubes.

Combine all the ingredients for the masala mix in a bowl and set aside.

Heat the oil in a large pan over a medium heat for 2–3 minutes. Check if the oil is hot enough by adding a few cumin seeds to the pan; if they start to sizzle, the oil is ready.

Once the oil is hot enough, lower the heat to low and add the cumin seeds. Stirring quickly and continuously, add the dried red chillies, cloves and cinnamon stick, then add the asafoetida. Tip the chana dal into the pan and use a spatula to coat the dal in the infused oil. Cover the pan with a lid and leave the dal to cook for 5 minutes.

Remove the lid, add 800 ml/ 3½ cups boiling water, stir again and cover to cook for a further 5 minutes.

Add the dhudhi and masala mix to the dal, mix thoroughly, cover and cook for a further 12–13 minutes, stirring occasionally. Check the dal is cooked by squeezing a piece in between your finger and thumb; it should be soft and crush easily. Insert a knife into the dhudhi; it should pierce easily.

Add the chopped tomatoes and lemon juice and cook for a final 3–4 minutes. Check the seasoning and, if required, add a little more salt to taste and turn off the heat. Garnish with coriander and serve with rotli and rice.

This curry can be stored in the fridge for up to 3 days. Reheat until piping hot before serving.

GILODA BATETA NU SHAAK
IVY GOURD & POTATO CURRY
(V) (GF) (NF)

Giloda (also known as tindora or ivy gourd) is a very popular vegetable in Gujarat. Many curries are prepared using this vegetable, but this simple version with potatoes is the most popular and my favourite. It's fairly easy to make, just make sure you prep the giloda, cut the potatoes and make the masala mix before starting to cook the curry. When shopping for giloda, look out for ones that are shiny, smooth and firm in texture.

650 g/1 lb. 7 oz. giloda (ivy gourd)
80 ml/⅓ cup sunflower oil
½ tablespoon cumin seeds
½ teaspoon asafoetida
6 garlic cloves, chopped
2 potatoes (or 1 large), peeled and sliced into chips/fries (I like to use Maris Piper)
chopped fresh coriander/cilantro, to garnish

MASALA MIX
1 tablespoon ground coriander
¾ teaspoon ground turmeric
1½ teaspoons red chilli/chile powder
1½ teaspoons salt

TO SERVE
Rotli (see page 86)
any rice dish of choice (see pages 99–100)
Gujarati Dal (see page 103)

SERVES 4

Combine all the ingredients for the masala mix in a bowl and set aside.

Wash and dry the giloda and trim the ends off each one. Cut each one lengthways into quarters or equal-sized pieces.

Heat the oil in a large pan over a high heat. Check if the oil is hot enough by adding a few cumin seeds to the oil; if they start to sizzle, the oil is ready.

Once the oil is hot enough, add the cumin seeds. As soon as they start to crackle, add the asafoetida, stir and add the garlic. Sauté until the garlic reaches a golden colour, stirring occasionally.

Add the giloda, turn the heat down to medium and cover the pan. Cook for 10–12 minutes, lift the lid every so often and give the vegetables a good stir. When you lift the lid, allow the water that has collected on the lid to drain back into the pan.

Add the potatoes and the masala mix to the pan and mix well, being careful not to break the potato pieces.

Cover and cook for a further 10–12 minutes until the potatoes and giloda are cooked through. If you like them softer, continue cooking for a bit longer.

Turn off the heat and leave to rest for 5 minutes, leaving the pan covered. Garnish with coriander and serve warm with rotli, rice and Gujarati Dal.

MAKAI NU SHAAK

CORN-ON-THE-COB CURRY

Ⓥ ⒼⒻ

This is a wonderful curry, best enjoyed when sweetcorn is in season. However, frozen corn works equally well; just defrost according to the instructions. You can also use corn kernels but the fun comes from eating the cob with your hands. Yes, it's messy eating! Use Rotli (see page 86) to mop up the sauce.

pinch of turmeric
pinch of red chilli/chile powder
pinch of salt
1 kg/2¼ lb. corn-on-the-cob,
    washed
120 ml/½ cup sunflower oil
½ tablespoon cumin seeds
¼ teaspoon asafoetida
2 onions, finely diced
4 garlic cloves, chopped
6 red tomatoes, blitzed into
    a purée/paste
½ teaspoon garam masala
¼ teaspoon granulated sugar
pinch of kasoori methi (dried
    fenugreek leaves), to garnish
Rotli (see page 86) or rice,
    to serve

MASALA MIX
20 g/scant ¼ cup unsalted
    peanuts
1 tablespoon Kashmiri chilli/chile
    powder
1 teaspoon red chilli/chile powder
⅓ teaspoon ground turmeric
½ tablespoon ground coriander
1 teaspoon ground cumin
1 teaspoon salt

SERVES 4

First, make the masala mix. Lightly toast the peanuts in a dry frying pan/skillet over a low flame until slightly charred. Set aside and leave to cool. Once cool, remove the skins, place in a food processor and grind the peanuts into a fine powder, taking care not to overprocess as they will become oily.

Place the ground peanuts into a bowl, add the remaining masala mix ingredients, mix together and set aside.

Place a saucepan of water over a high heat and add a pinch of turmeric, red chilli powder and salt. Bring the water to the boil. Add the corn cobs, cover the pan, reduce the heat and simmer for 8–10 minutes or until the corn is cooked.

Use a slotted spoon to remove the corn cobs from the water and set aside until they are cool enough to handle. Do not discard the corn cooking water. Place the corn cobs on a cutting board and chop them into 3–4-cm/1¼–1½-in. pieces.

Heat the oil in a large frying pan/skillet over a medium heat for several minutes. Add the cumin seeds and once they start to crackle, add the asafoetida and onions. Stir well and add the garlic.

Cook until the onions turn a lightly golden colour, then add the masala mix. Stir well and cook for several minutes.

Add a drizzle of cold water and then add the tomato purée. Turn up the heat to high and cook, stirring occasionally. After 2–3 minutes, add the garam masala and sugar and stir. Cook until the oil separates.

Add the corn pieces to the pan along with 240 ml/1 cup of the reserved corn cooking water. Cover and cook for 5 minutes. Turn off the heat and leave to rest for a few minutes.

Garnish with a pinch of kasoori methi and serve with Rotli (and with rice if you are using loose corn kernels).

TIP *If you are reheating this curry, add 240 ml/1 cup water and heat until piping hot. The gravy will thicken as it cools.*

VALOR RINGAR NU SHAAK

HYACINTH BEAN CURRY

(V) (GF) (NF)

This is an authentic curry with a distinctive taste. It may not appeal to everyone but I encourage you to give it a go. Also called hyacinth beans, valor grow in India and East Africa, and can be bought from Asian grocery shops all year round. We recommend buying them fresh and using them on the day they are bought. Valor pods contain between two and four firm beans. The pods are tender and so we use both the pods and the beans in this dish. Make sure you remove as much of the fibrous strings from the valor as possible. This curry is normally served with Shrikhand (see page 160).

250 g/9 oz. fresh valor
   (hyacinth beans)
50 ml/3½ tablespoons sunflower
   oil
1 tablespoon carom seeds
½ teaspoon asafoetida
250 g/9 oz. aubergine/eggplant,
   chopped into bite-sized pieces
½ teaspoon salt
½ teaspoon ground turmeric
2 teaspoons ground coriander
1 teaspoon ground cumin
2 teaspoons red chilli/chile
   powder
handful of chopped fresh
   coriander/cilantro, to garnish

TO SERVE
Rotli (see page 86)
Gujarati Dal (see page 103)
Shrikhand (see page 160)

SERVES 4

Place the beans in a colander and rinse under cold water. Leave to drain, then use a clean dish towel to dry the beans.

Take each pod, break the top with your fingers and pull downwards to remove the vein on the side. Now break the bottom and pull upwards to remove the vein on the other side. Pull the pod apart to open and cut in half, removing any veins left behind. Do this with each pod.

Heat the sunflower oil in a pan over a medium heat for 2 minutes. Check if the oil is hot enough by dropping in a few carom seeds; if they sizzle, the oil is ready.

Add the carom seeds to the pan, give them a quick stir, then add the asafoetida. Add the prepared beans and stir well so that everything is coated in the spiced oil. Cover the pan and continue to cook for 2 minutes.

Lift the lid and give the beans a stir. Add the aubergine, salt, turmeric, coriander, cumin and chilli powder. Give everything a stir to mix the spices into the beans and aubergine. Cover the pan and continue cooking.

Every so often, lift the lid allowing the water from the lid to drain back into the curry. Give the veg a quick mix and cover again – do this for 2–3 minutes. Once the aubergine is soft, remove the curry from the heat and serve with the chopped coriander to garnish.

Serve with Rotli, Gujarati Dal and Shrikhand. If you are not serving the curry straight away, store it, keep in the fridge in an airtight container for up to 3 days, then reheat until piping hot before serving.

NOTE *This is a gluten-free curry but do check the label on asafoetida; gluten is sometimes used in the manufacturing process.*

BHARELA RINGER NU SHAAK
AUBERGINE & POTATO CURRY
(V) (GF)

This is a lovely fragrant curry; the aubergine/eggplant and potatoes hold the spice mix really well. Baby aubergines have quite a firm texture, but any aubergine will work in this dish.

7–8 baby aubergines/eggplant
12 baby potatoes
120 ml/½ cup sunflower oil
½ tablespoon cumin seeds
½ teaspoon asafoetida
fresh coriander/cilantro sprigs,
    to garnish

MASALA MIX
50 g/½ cup unsalted peanuts,
    roasted, skin removed and
    ground into crumbs
    (see page 54)
1 teaspoon ground turmeric
½ tablespoon red chilli/chile
    powder
3 tablespoons ground coriander
1 teaspoon garam masala
3 tablespoons caster/granulated
    sugar
1 teaspoon salt
½ teaspoon cumin seeds
2 teaspoons Ginger, Garlic and
    Chilli Paste (see page 14)

TO SERVE
Rotli (see page 86)
Gujarati Dal (see page 103)
Bataku (see page 143)

SERVES 4

Combine all the ingredients for the masala mix in a bowl and set aside.

Take an aubergine and trim any excess leaves around the edge but don't cut off the top. Turn the aubergine on its side and trim the tip off the bottom. Now turn again so the aubergine is upside down and carefully cut the aubergine lengthways into quarters, but do not cut all the way up, so the quarters remain attached at the stem. Place the aubergines in a bowl of cold water. Repeat until all the aubergines have been prepared.

Take a baby potato and cut along the middle to just over half the depth of the potato. Use your knife to gently push the potato apart but be careful not to split it into two; don't worry too much if it happens though! Repeat until all the potatoes have been prepared.

Use your fingers to gently fill the aubergines with the spice mix. Press down and push the mix into the cuts. Once the aubergine is generously stuffed, press all four sides back together. Place on a plate and repeat until all the aubergines have been stuffed.

Gently fill each potato the same way as the aubergines until all the potatoes are stuffed. Press the sides of the potatoes together. You will have some spice mix left over; set aside to use later.

Place a large pan over a low heat for 2–3 minutes. Add the oil

and heat for 2 minutes. Check if the oil is hot enough by adding a few cumin seeds to the pan; if they sizzle and pop, the oil is ready.

Add the cumin seeds and asafoetida and then immediately add the stuffed potatoes, placing them cut sides upwards to keep the masala mix in. Cover and turn up the heat to medium.

After 1 minute, gently raise the pan off the hob/stove and, keeping the lid on, shake the potatoes upwards. Return the pan to the heat. Again, after 1 minute, repeat the shaking, then repeat once more after another minute (so a total of 3 minutes cooking and shaking). Lift the lid, shake the potatoes and carefully add the aubergines to the pan. Cover and turn down the heat to low.

Let the curry cook for about 3 minutes, then shake again with the lid on. Every so often, lift the lid, allowing the water from the lid to drain back into the curry, shake from side to side and upwards, then replace the lid and let it cook. Continue cooking until the potatoes are soft. Add the remainder of the masala mix to the curry, cover and shake well. Turn off the heat and let the curry rest for 3–4 minutes. Garnish with coriander sprigs.

As this is a dry curry with no sauce, it is best served with Rotli, Gujarati Dal and Bataku.

KORU BATETA NU SHAAK
DRY POTATO CURRY

(V) (GF)

This dry potato curry is one the most popular Gujarati curries. When Hindus fast there are certain foods that can be eaten. The list of foods allowed is often referred to as *farari* food and includes all the fruits, nuts and milk products. It also includes potatoes. I make this dish for my eldest son, Jaymin, who fasts every Monday. This curry is very easy to make and tastes great! I've used cashews in this recipe, but peanuts work well too. The sesame seeds add a lovely flavour to this dish.

5 large potatoes
   (about 1 kg/2¼ lb.)
200 ml/scant 1 cup sunflower oil
2 teaspoons cumin seeds
2 teaspoons mustard seeds
2 teaspoons sesame seeds
½ teaspoon asafoetida
2 green chillies/chilis, finely
   chopped
12–14 curry leaves
2 tablespoons sultanas/golden
   raisins
2 tablespoons cashews
1 teaspoon ground turmeric
1 teaspoon salt
1 teaspoon red chilli/chile powder
2 teaspoons ground coriander
1 teaspoon ground cumin
2 tablespoons caster/granulated
   sugar
handful of chopped fresh
   coriander/cilantro, to garnish

TO SERVE
plain yogurt (omit or use a
   plant-based yogurt if vegan)
   or Gujarati Dal (see page 103)
your choice of rice dish
   (see pages 99–100)

SERVES 4

Boil the potatoes with their skins on in a large saucepan of salted water until tender. Check they are done by inserting a sharp knife into a potato; it should fall off the knife easily. Drain and set the potatoes aside until cool enough to handle. Use your hands to peel away the skins, then use your hands to break the potatoes into large chunks.

Heat the oil in a large pan over a medium heat. Check to see if the oil is hot enough by adding a few cumin seeds; if they sizzle, the oil is ready.

Turn down the heat to low. Add the cumin, mustard and sesame seeds. Stir quickly and add the asafoetida, green chillies and curry leaves. Fry gently for 1 minute, then add the sultanas and cashews and fry for a further 1 minute.

Add the potatoes to the pan and turn up the heat to medium. Shake the pan to gently mix and fry for 1 minute. Add the rest of the ingredients, stir gently to mix, then cover the pan. Cook for a few minutes until the potatoes turn a light golden colour. Remove from the heat and garnish with the chopped coriander.

Serve with plain yogurt or Gujarati Dal and rice.

If you are not serving the curry straight away, store it in the fridge in an airtight container for up to 3 days, then reheat until piping hot before serving.

MATAR PANEER

PEA & PANEER CURRY

This dish is a family favourite. Paneer is versatile, cooks quickly, is similar
to halloumi in texture and does not disintegrate when simmered in sauces.
I know recipes with a long list of ingredients can be off-putting, but do try
this one; the recipe itself is not complicated and the result is so worth it!

5 tomatoes, chopped
2 green chillies/chilis
3–4-cm/1¼–1½-in. long piece
   of fresh ginger, peeled
400 g/14 oz. paneer, cut into
   bite-sized cubes
60 ml/¼ cup sunflower oil
1 tablespoon ghee
1 teaspoon cumin seeds
1 dried red chilli/chili, broken
   into pieces
2 bay leaves
2 cloves
3-cm/1¼-in. long cinnamon
   stick, broken into pieces
⅓ teaspoon asafoetida
1 onion, finely chopped
½ tablespoon Ginger and
   Garlic Paste (see page 14)
⅛ teaspoon ground turmeric
⅓ teaspoon red chilli/chile
   powder
1 teaspoon Kashmiri chilli/
   chile powder
1 teaspoon ground coriander
½ teaspoon ground cumin
½ teaspoon garam masala
½ teaspoon salt
200 g/1⅓ cups fresh peas
   (defrosted if using frozen)
1 teaspoon kasoori methi
   (dried fenugreek leaves)
handful of chopped fresh
   coriander/cilantro

TO SERVE
Rotli (see page 86)
your choice of rice dish
   (see pages 99–100)

SERVES 4

Place the tomatoes, green chillies
and ginger in a blender and blitz
to a smooth paste.

Heat a drizzle of oil in a frying
pan/skillet over a medium heat.
Once the oil is hot, add the paneer
and shallow fry on all sides until
lightly golden. Remove the paneer
from the pan and set aside.

Place the pan back over a
medium heat and add the oil and
ghee. Once the ghee has melted,
add the cumin seeds, dried red
chilli, bay leaves, cloves, cinnamon
stick and asafoetida. Mix into the
oil and cook for 2 minutes.

Add the onion and sauté for
6–7 minutes, or until golden brown
in colour.

Add the ginger and garlic
paste, cook for 1 minute, then
add the turmeric, red chilli powder,
Kashmiri chilli powder, coriander,
cumin, garam masala and salt. Add
a drizzle of water and cook for
1–2 minutes, stirring continuously.

Add the blended tomato paste
and turn up the heat to high. Cover
and cook for 1 minute, then add the
peas and 200 ml/scant 1 cup water
(add more if you want the gravy
to be more liquid). Give everything
a good stir, cover and cook for
3–4 minutes, stirring occasionally.

Lower the heat to medium, and
add the paneer. Stirring occasionally,
cook for 3–4 minutes or until the
oil separates.

Add the kasoori methi and
chopped coriander, stir and serve
with Rotli and rice.

BATETA NU SHAAK
POTATO CURRY

(V) (GF)

Bateta nu shaak simply means potato curry in Gujarati. This curry is a staple of every Gujarati household and there are many versions of it. Peanuts are known as sing dana in Gujarati and are used in a variety of recipes. I've added peanuts to the potatoes in this recipe to add an extra depth of flavour. Leave out the peanuts, if you need to, as the dish works just as well without them.

5 large potatoes, peeled and cut into 3-cm/1¼-in. cubes
50 g/½ cup unsalted peanuts
1 onion, roughly chopped
90 ml/generous ⅓ cup sunflower oil
1 teaspoon cumin seeds
⅓ teaspoon asafoetida
1 teaspoon Ginger and Garlic Paste (see page 14)
1 tablespoon Kashmiri chilli/chile powder
½ teaspoon red chilli/chile powder
½ tablespoon ground coriander
¼ teaspoon ground turmeric
½ teaspoon garam masala
½ teaspoon salt
3 tomatoes, chopped
2 tablespoons tomato purée/paste
1 tablespoon granulated sugar

TO SERVE
Rotli (see page 86)
your choice of rice dish (see pages 99–100)
Bataku (see page 143)

SERVES 4

Cook the potatoes in a saucepan of boiling water until soft. Check if they are cooked by inserting a sharp knife into a piece of potato; it should fall off the knife easily. Drain and set aside.

Place a frying pan/skillet over a low heat, add the peanuts and dry roast, stirring continuously, until the peanut skins start to darken. Remove from the heat and set aside on a plate until cool enough to handle. Remove the skins by rubbing the peanuts in between your hands, then place the nuts in a food processor or blender. Grind the peanuts to a breadcrumb consistency. Remove and set aside.

Add the onion to the food processor and blitz to a paste.

Add the oil to a saucepan over a medium heat. When hot, add the cumin seeds, and once they crackle, add the asafoetida and blended onions. Sauté until the onions turn a lightly yellow colour, stirring occasionally.

Add the ginger and garlic paste, stir to mix well, then add the Kashmiri chilli powder and red chilli powder. Cook for 1–2 minutes. Mix well and add the peanuts and potatoes. Mix to coat the potatoes with the spices, then add the ground coriander, turmeric, garam masala and salt and stir well. Cook for 2 minutes.

Add the chopped tomatoes, tomato purée, sugar and 240 ml/1 cup water and mix well. Cover, stirring occasionally, and cook for 4–5 minutes or until the potatoes are cooked through. Check the seasoning and adjust the salt, sugar and chilli powder as needed.

Serve with Rotli, rice and your favourite sides.

SHAHI PANEER
MILD PANEER CURRY

80 ml/⅓ cup sunflower oil

2 tablespoons unsalted butter

1 teaspoon cumin seeds

½ tablespoon Kashmiri chilli/ chile powder

½ teaspoon red chilli/chile powder

¼ teaspoon ground turmeric

½ tablespoon ground coriander

½ tablespoon ground cumin

½ teaspoon salt

⅓ teaspoon garam masala

400 g/14 oz. paneer, cut into cubes and fried until golden on all sides

50 ml/scant ¼ cup double/heavy cream

1 tablespoon kasoori methi (dried fenugreek leaves)

Rotli (see page 86) or rice (see page 99), to serve

MASALA MIX

2 bay leaves

1 dried red chilli/chili

5 green cardamom pods

1 black cardamon pod

1-cm/½-in. long cinnamon stick

1 star anise

2 cloves

5 black peppercorns

GRAVY BASE

2 tablespoons sunflower oil

2 tablespoons unsalted butter

1 onion, finely sliced

4–5-cm/1½–2-in. piece of fresh ginger, peeled and chopped

5–6 garlic cloves, chopped

1 green chilli/chili, finely chopped

50 g/scant ½ cup cashews

4 red tomatoes, chopped

240 ml/1 cup hot water

SERVES 4

This dish originates from the Mogul era and hence is known as a royal dish. It's a beautifully rich, flavourful curry using cashews and cream, but if you want to make it vegan simply skip the butter, use firm tofu instead of paneer and use vegan cream instead of double/heavy cream. This dish is perfect for special occasions or when guests come over for dinner.

Combine all the ingredients for the masala mix in a bowl and set aside.

To make the gravy base, heat the oil and butter in a wide pan over a medium heat. Once the butter has melted, add the masala mix and cook for 1–2 minutes.

Add the onions, mix well and sauté for 2–3 minutes, stirring occasionally. Add the ginger, garlic and chilli and fry for 2–3 minutes.

Add the cashews and tomatoes and mix well. Add the hot water and cook for 4–5 minutes until the tomatoes are soft. Remove the pan from the heat and spread the gravy base over a plate to cool. Remove the bay leaves, cinnamon stick, green cardamom, black cardamom and star anise from the gravy base and discard.

Transfer the gravy base to a blender, add 60 ml/¼ cup water and blitz to a smooth paste. Strain into a bowl to remove any lumps.

To make the curry, heat the oil and butter in a frying pan/skillet over a high heat. Once the butter has melted, add the cumin seeds.

When the cumin seeds start to crackle, add the Kashmiri chilli powder, red chilli powder and a drizzle of water to help loosen everything.

Add the turmeric, coriander, cumin, salt and garam masala and mix well. Heat for 1 minute, then add the gravy base to the pan with a drizzle of water. Cover and heat for 3–4 minutes, stirring occasionally.

Reduce the heat to low, add the paneer and cover. Every so often, lift the lid, allowing the water from the lid to drip back into the pan and stir.

When the oil separates, add the cream and stir into the curry. Gently simmer for 2–3 minutes, add the kasoori methi and remove from the heat.

Serve with rotli and rice.

If you are not serving the curry straight away, store it in the fridge in an airtight container for up to 3 days, then reheat until piping hot before serving.

GUVAR NU SHAAK
CLUSTER BEAN CURRY
(V) (GF) (NF)

Guvar nu shaak is a simple but delicious guvar (cluster bean) curry, requiring only the most basic Indian spices. Try to find tender guvar as they can be a tough vegetable. The cooking time will vary according to the toughness of your beans. They are available from Asian grocery shops, but try to buy fresh guvar rather than using frozen ones. The beans are slightly bitter and so to counteract this, add a sweetener such as palm sugar/jaggery or granulated sugar to the curry to taste if needed.

400 g/14 oz. guvar (cluster beans)
60 ml/¼ cup sunflower oil
1 teaspoon carom seeds
⅓ teaspoon asafoetida
4 garlic cloves, chopped
1 teaspoon ground turmeric
1 teaspoon red chilli/chile powder
2 teaspoons ground coriander
½ teaspoon salt
150 ml/⅔ cup canned chopped
　　tomatoes
⅛ teaspoon garam masala

TO SERVE
Rotli (see page 86)
your choice of rice dish
　　(see pages 99–100)
Gujarati Dal (see page 103)
plain yogurt with a pinch of chilli/
　　chile powder and cumin seeds
　　(omit or use a plant-based
　　yogurt if vegan)

SERVES 2

Wash the guvar in cold water. Top and tail each bean to remove the ends and then cut each in two.

Heat the oil in a saucepan over a high heat for 2 minutes. Check the oil is hot enough by dropping a few carom seeds into the oil; if they sizzle, the oil is ready.

Add the carom seeds and once they start to crackle, add the asafoetida and garlic, then reduce the heat to low.

Add the guvar and stir well to coat the beans in the spiced oil. Cook for 1–2 minutes, then add the turmeric, red chilli powder, coriander and salt.

Mix well, cover the pan and cook for a further 15 minutes, stirring every so often.

Lift the lid, add 50 ml/scant ¼ cup water, stir the guvar and cover again. Guvar can be tough, so you may need to add a little extra water to cook the beans through.

After 3 minutes, stir in the chopped tomatoes and add another 50 ml/scant ¼ cup water.

Add the garam masala, cover and cook for a further 2–3 minutes until the guvar are tender.

Serve with rotli, rice, Gujarati Dal and yogurt.

TIPS *You can make a variation on this curry by adding boiled potatoes at the same time as adding the tomatoes near the end of the cooking process.*

If you struggle to find guvar, use fine green beans instead.

GOBI MATAR NU SHAAK
CAULIFLOWER & PEA CURRY
(V) (GF) (NF)

This cauliflower and pea curry is very popular in Gujarat and North India. In Gujarati, *gobi* means cauliflower and *matar* means peas. This curry is quick and easy to make using just peas and cauliflower, which absorb the spices really well. I make this dish regularly at home and especially if I'm in a rush. It's quite a dry curry so I serve it with some dal or Raita (see page 136), fresh Rotli (see page 86) and rice (see pages 99–100). I try to use fresh garden peas, which do require time to separate the peas from their pods. However, if I can't get hold of any or I'm short on time, I use frozen peas instead.

1 large cauliflower
250 g/2 cups fresh peas
    (defrosted if using frozen)
120 ml/½ cup sunflower oil
1 teaspoon cumin seeds
¼ teaspoon asafoetida
1 dried red chilli/chili
½ red (bell) pepper, deseeded
    and cut into cubes
½ teaspoon ground turmeric
1 teaspoon red chilli/chile powder
2 teaspoons ground coriander
½ teaspoon salt
handful of chopped fresh
    coriander/cilantro, to garnish

SERVES 4

Trim the leaves from the cauliflower, then separate the florets from the stalk. Halve each floret down the middle. Fill a large saucepan with hot water, add a pinch of salt and submerge the cut florets in the water. Leave for 5 minutes, then drain.

Place a saucepan over a medium heat, add the sunflower oil and heat for 1–2 minutes. Check if the oil is hot enough by adding a few cumin seeds to the pan; if they start to sizzle and crackle, the oil is ready.

Once the oil is hot enough, turn down the heat to low and add the cumin seeds, asafoetida, dried red chilli and cauliflower florets. Stir to coat the florets with the spiced oil, then cover and cook for 5–6 minutes, stirring occasionally.

Add the peas and red pepper to the pan, then add the remaining spices and salt. Mix gently to coat the veg with the spices as much as possible, then cover the pan. After 2–3 minutes, lift the lid and stir well. Cook uncovered and stir occasionally for a further 2 minutes, or until the cauliflower is cooked through. Remove the pan from the heat. Garnish with the chopped coriander and serve.

If you are not serving the curry straight away, store it in the fridge in an airtight container for up to 3 days, then reheat until piping hot before serving.

BHINDA BATETA NU SHAAK

OKRA & POTATO CURRY

(V) (GF) (NF)

This okra and potato curry is more of a dry, stir-fried curry than a gravy-based curry. It's a delicate dish for which the potatoes are cut into small cubes so they cook quickly. This Gujarati classic is very popular with our guests in the restaurant. My sons didn't really like okra when they were younger, but they absolutely love them now. I always use fresh okra, which are readily available.

100 ml/generous ⅓ cup
   sunflower oil
1 teaspoon carom seeds
½ teaspoon asafoetida
200 g/7 oz. okra, washed, dried
   and cut widthways into
   1.5-cm/½-in. pieces
200 g/7 oz. waxy white potatoes,
   peeled and cut into 1.5-cm/
   ½-in. cubes
1 teaspoon ground turmeric
1 teaspoon red chilli/chile powder
2 teaspoons ground coriander
⅔ teaspoon salt
¼ teaspoon lemon juice

TO SERVE
Rotli (see page 86)
Gujarati Dal (see page 103)

SERVES 2

Heat the oil in a frying pan/skillet over a high heat for about 2 minutes. Check the oil is hot enough by dropping a few carom seeds into the pan; if they sizzle, the oil is ready.

Lower the heat to medium. Add the carom seeds and asafoetida to the pan, stir once and then add the okra. Stir to coat the okra in the oil, cover the pan and cook for 2 minutes, stirring occasionally.

Add the potato, stir a couple of times and then add the turmeric, red chilli powder, coriander, salt and lemon juice. Stir to coat the vegetables in the spices.

Cover and cook for about 8–10 minutes. Occasionally lift the lid allowing the water from the lid to drain back down into the pan, stir and replace the lid. Once the okra and potato can be cut easily, remove from the heat.

Serve with rotli and Gujarati Dal if liked.

TIP *It is essential that the okra is dry prior to, and during, the cooking process. Wash the okra whole, pat dry and remove the stems before slicing and cooking. This ensures the okra will not become slimy during cooking.*

DAL PALAK
MOONG DAL & SPINACH CURRY
(V) (GF) (NF)

This is comfort food at its finest! Dal palak is a very famous, healthy North Indian dish made with moong dal, spinach and spices. It is easy to prepare as the moong dal cooks more quickly than other dals. I eat dal palak often, as it's not only delicious but has high nutritional values and health benefits. It gives balance to my diet and is easy to digest too. Serve this lovely dish on cold evenings or when you are feeling poorly.

150 g/¾ cup moong dal
60 ml/¼ cup sunflower oil
½ tablespoon cumin seeds
½ teaspoon asafoetida
4 garlic cloves, chopped
⅛ teaspoon ground turmeric
1 teaspoon ground coriander
¼ teaspoon red chilli/chile powder
½ teaspoon Ginger and Garlic Paste (see page 14)
½ teaspoon salt
1 green chilli/chili, chopped
150 g/5½ oz. baby spinach, chopped

TO SERVE
Rotli (see page 86) or your choice of rice dish (see pages 99–100)

SERVES 2

Wash the dal in cold water and then soak in a bowl with 1 litre/4 cups cold water for 2–3 hours. Rinse in fresh water before using.

Heat the oil in a wide pan over a high heat for 2 minutes. Add the cumin seeds and once they start to crackle, add the asafoetida and garlic and stir well. Reduce the heat to medium.

Add the dal and stir to coat in the spiced oil. Add 750 ml/3 cups water, stir quickly and then add all the other ingredients, except the spinach. Cover and cook for about 18–20 minutes, stirring occasionally, until the dal is cooked through. To check, take a piece of dal and squeeze in between your finger and thumb; it should crush easily.

If the dal is too dry, add a little water to loosen.

Add the spinach, turn off the heat and cover for 2–3 minutes before serving.

Serve with Rotli or rice.

If you are not serving the curry straight away, store it in the fridge in an airtight container for up to 3 days, then reheat until piping hot before serving.

TIPS *As the spinach cooks very fast, add it right at the end of the cooking process and let it wilt in the hot pan before serving.*

As a variation, kale can be used instead of spinach.

CHANA MASALA
CHICKPEA CURRY
(V) (GF) (NF)

I want to introduce you to one of Northern India's most popular vegan curries – chana masala. A renowned classic and incredibly popular in this region, it's a hearty, wholesome dish in which chickpeas/garbanzo beans, or chana, are cooked in a delicious tomato and onion sauce with a simple spice blend 'masala'.

100 ml/scant ½ cup sunflower oil
½ tablespoon carom seeds
½ teaspoon asafoetida
1 dried red chilli/chili
1 large white onion, diced
4 garlic cloves, chopped
1 tablespoon chickpea/gram flour
4 tomatoes, blitzed to a purée/
    paste in a blender
1 tablespoon Kashmiri chilli/chile
    powder
1 teaspoon red chilli/chile powder
½ tablespoon ground coriander
⅓ teaspoon ground turmeric
1 teaspoon salt
1 tablespoon palm sugar/jaggery
½ teaspoon garam masala
2 x 400-g/14-oz. cans chickpeas/
    garbanzo beans, drained
your choice of rice dish (see
    pages 99–100), to serve

TO GARNISH
sliced red onions
lemon wedges
sliced green chilli/chili
fresh coriander/cilantro leaves

SERVES 4

Heat the oil in a frying pan/skillet over a high heat for 2 minutes. Add the carom seeds and once they start to crackle, add the asafoetida and dried chilli. Stir the oil quickly, add the onions and sauté in the oil until lightly golden in colour, stirring occasionally.

Add the garlic and lower the heat to the lowest setting. Add the chickpea flour and stir quickly to mix well. Add the tomatoes and raise the heat to high again. Cover the pan and cook, stirring occasionally.

Once the oil separates from the onions, add the Kashmiri powder and red chilli powder and mix well. Cover and heat for 1 minute, then add the coriander, turmeric and salt. Mix into the curry and then add the palm sugar and garam masala along with 120 ml/½ cup water.

Add the chickpeas to the curry, mixing well. Cover and cook for about 5 minutes or until the oil has separated and the curry is piping hot.

Serve with rice and garnish with red onions, lemon wedges, sliced chilli and coriander.

If you are not serving the curry straight away, store it in the fridge in an airtight container for up to 3 days, then reheat until piping hot before serving.

TIPS *For ease, I use canned chickpeas in this recipe. However, dried chickpeas can be used instead. Just make sure to soak them for a few hours, ideally overnight before using them as instructed.*

I've also added a little chickpea/ gram flour to this recipe to thicken the sauce.

CHANA DAL
YELLOW SPLIT PEA CURRY

(V) (GF) (NF)

I absolutely love to cook this dish when I'm in the mood for something warm and savoury; it's great on cold winter evenings. There are three stages to this dish. The dal requires a bit of prepping as it needs to be washed, soaked and then cooked in a pressure cooker. Once the dal is ready, it's cooked with spices and, finally, a vagar (flavoured oil) is added to the dish.

100 g/generous ½ cup chana dal (yellow split peas)
1 litre/4 cups just boiled water
⅛ teaspoon salt
⅛ teaspoon ground turmeric

DAL
120 ml/½ cup sunflower oil
1 teaspoon cumin seeds
1 dried red chilli/chili
3–4-cm/1¼–1½-in. long cinnamon stick, broken into pieces
2 cloves
2 bay leaves
⅛ teaspoon ground turmeric
⅓ teaspoon asafoetida
1 onion, finely diced
1 tablespoon Ginger and Garlic Paste (see page 14)
2 green chillies/chilis, chopped
120 ml/½ cup canned chopped tomatoes
½ tablespoon Kashmiri chilli/chile powder
½ teaspoon ground coriander
¼ teaspoon ground cumin
¼ teaspoon garam masala
½ teaspoon salt

VAGAR (TEMPERED OIL)
2 tablespoons sunflower oil
½ teaspoon mustard seeds
1 red chilli/chili, sliced in half
4–5 curry leaves

TO SERVE
Rotli (see page 86) or rice
Limbu nu Athanu (see page 148)

SERVES 2

Wash the chana dal several times under cold running water until the water runs clear. Place the dal in a bowl, add 500 ml/2 cups just boiled water and soak for 15 minutes. Drain the al and set aside.

Pour 500 ml/2 cups water into a pressure cooker and add the soaked dal, salt and turmeric. Close the lid and place over a high heat. Cook until the pressure cooker whistles twice, remove from the heat and set aside to cool.

Without opening the lid, lift the whistle to release any pressure and then open the pressure cooker. Check the dal is ready by squeezing a piece of dal in between your finger and thumb; it should crush easily. If the dal is still hard, close the lid and return to a high heat for 1 more whistle.

Heat the oil in a pan over a medium heat for 2 minutes. Check if the oil is hot enough by placing a few cumin seeds into the pan; if they sizzle, the oil is ready.

Add the cumin seeds, dried red chilli, cinnamon sticks, cloves and bay leaves and stir quickly a couple of times. Add the turmeric and asafoetida, stir quickly to mix and then add the onion. Stirring occasionally, cook the onion for about 8 minutes, or until it turns a lovely golden-brown colour.

Add the ginger and garlic paste, stir to mix and then add the green chillies. Once the paste starts to turn a light golden colour, add the tomatoes and stir for 2 minutes, crushing any lumps of tomatoes as you stir.

Stir the Kashmiri chilli powder into the mixture. Add the ground coriander, cumin, garam masala and salt and mix well for 2 minutes.

Add the cooked dal to the pan along with the cooking water, raise the heat to high, cover and cook, stirring occasionally, for about 3–4 minutes.

Remove the pan from the heat and transfer the dal to a dish.

At the last minute make the vagar. Clean the pan you were using with paper towels. Heat the oil in the pan over a high heat. Add the mustard seeds and when they start to crackle, add the red chilli and curry leaves. Stir quickly and then immediately pour the vagar over the chana dal.

Serve with Rotli, rice and any other side dishes such as Limbu nu Athanu.

TIPS *This dal is delicious garnished with micro coriander/cilantro and red amaranth if liked.*

See page 82 for instructions for how to cook the dal if you don't have a pressure cooker.

PURVAR NU SHAAK
POINTED GOURD CURRY
(GF) (NF)

This is a wonderful Gujarati curry using purvar (pointed gourd). They are slightly tougher than other gourds, which makes stuffing purvar with a masala mix ideal as it holds the filling well. When cooking purvar, make sure not to stir them in the pan – shake the pan gently from side to side instead. The masala mix adds an extra depth of flavour to this dish.

350 g/12½ oz. purvar
  (pointed gourd)
100 ml/scant ½ cup sunflower oil
1 teaspoon cumin seeds
80 ml/⅓ cup plain yogurt
1 teaspoon ground coriander
1 teaspoon Kashmiri chilli/chile
  powder
¼ teaspoon ground turmeric
1 teaspoon ground cumin
¼ teaspoon asafoetida
4 tomatoes, chopped
½ teaspoon red chilli/chile powder
1 teaspoon granulated sugar

MASALA MIX
6 tablespoons ground coriander
½ teaspoon ground turmeric
2 teaspoons ground cumin
1 teaspoon Kashmiri chilli/chile
  powder
½ teaspoon salt
½ teaspoon asafoetida
½ teaspoon garam masala
2 tablespoons chickpea/gram flour
handful of fresh coriander/
  cilantro leaves
½ teaspoon fresh lemon juice
1 tablespoon Ginger and Garlic
  Paste (see page 14)
1 tablespoon sunflower oil
handful of fresh coriander/
  cilantro sprigs, to garnish

TO SERVE
Rotli (see page 86) and rice

SERVES 2

Combine all the masala mix ingredients in a bowl until it all comes together. If you squeeze the masala mix, it should hold its shape.

Wash, peel and top and tail the purvar. Make a slit down the sides of each purvar and scoop out all the seeds from inside. Gently open each purvar, ensuring they don't split open completely, and stuff each one with the masala mix. Press and squeeze the sides together and remove any excess stuffing as needed. Once each purvar has been filled, set aside any remaining masala mix for later.

Heat the oil in a wide pan over a high heat for 1 minute. Add the cumin seeds and once they start to crackle, turn the heat to low.

Add the purvar with the stuffed side facing upwards so the masala mix doesn't fall out. Cover the pan and cook for 5–6 minutes. Check the purvar are ready by using a fork to pierce the purvar; it should slide easily off.

Once cooked, transfer the purvar to a plate, leaving any oil and masala mix left behind in the pan.

Place the yogurt, coriander, Kashmiri chilli powder and turmeric in a bowl and mix together. If you have any masala mix left over from stuffing the purvar, add this to the yogurt mixture too.

Place the same cooking pan back over a low heat. Once the oil has heated again, add the cumin and asafoetida and mix well. Add the chopped tomatoes and stir well.

Once the oil separates from the other ingredients, add the red chilli powder, stir quickly and add the yogurt mixture to the pan. Gently mix together.

Once the oil separates again, add 2 tablespoons water and cook for a further 2–3 minutes, stirring occasionally.

When the mixture thickens add the sugar, stir well and turn off the heat. Return the purvar to the pan and gently stir into the sauce. Cover and leave for 5 minutes. Garnish with a few coriander sprigs.

Serve with rice and Rotli.

TIP *When selecting purvar, buy the young ones with bright green skins and white lines running down their length. They resemble small watermelons!*

RAJMA NU SHAAK

KIDNEY BEAN CURRY

(V) (GF) (NF)

This dish is so full of flavour that it's worth the time it takes to soak and cook the dried kidney beans in a pressure cooker before making the curry. However, you can skip the first two stages if you use canned kidney beans instead, making this curry just as quick to cook as any other.

TO PREPARE THE BEANS
160 g/1 cup dried kidney beans
700 ml/scant 3 cups boiling water
pinch of salt

CURRY
50 ml/scant ¼ cup sunflower oil
½ tablespoon carom seeds
¼ teaspoon asafoetida
1 teaspoon chickpea/gram flour
250 ml/1½ cups canned chopped
    tomatoes
¼ teaspoon ground turmeric
1 teaspoon ground coriander
½ teaspoon ground cumin
½ teaspoon salt
¼ teaspoon red chilli/chile
    powder
½ teaspoon Ginger, Garlic
    and Chilli Paste (see page 14)
½ teaspoon garam masala
2 teaspoons granulated sugar
2 tablespoons tomato ketchup
chopped fresh coriander/cilantro,
    to garnish

TO SERVE
Rotli (see page 86)
your choice of rice dish
    (see pages 99–100)

SERVES 4

TIP *If you are using canned kidney beans, make sure you drain and wash them thoroughly before use.*

Place the dried kidney beans in a bowl and add the boiling water. Set aside and leave to soak for 6–8 hours but preferably overnight. When ready, drain the kidney beans in a sieve/strainer and wash them thoroughly under hot running water from the tap.

Place 450 ml/1¾ cups water in a pressure cooker with the salt. Heat until the water starts to simmer, then add the kidney beans. Close the lid and cook until the pressure cooker whistles 3–4 times.

Remove from the heat and set aside to cool. Without opening the lid, lift the whistle to release any pressure and then open the pressure cooker. Check if the kidney beans are cooked by pressing a bean in between your finger and thumb; if it crushes easily, the beans are ready. If the beans are still not cooked properly, return the pressure cooker to the heat until the cooker whistles once.

Heat the oil in a saucepan over a medium heat for 90 seconds. Check if the oil is hot enough by placing a few carom seeds into the pan; if they sizzle, the oil is ready, otherwise heat for a further 30 seconds and check again.

Add the carom seeds to the oil and stir for 30 seconds. Add the asafoetida, mix quickly, then add the chickpea flour. Reduce the heat to a low heat and mix quickly until the flour turns a slightly red colour.

Add 240 ml/1 cup water and the chopped tomatoes and stir gently for 2 minutes. Add the turmeric, coriander, cumin, salt, chilli powder and ginger, garlic and chilli paste and stir until all the flavours are combined. Add the garam masala and stir for a further 30 seconds.

Add the cooked kidney beans and tomato ketchup and stir until the curry comes to a simmer. Cover and cook for another couple of minutes.

Remove the lid and take the pan off the heat. Leave the curry to cool slightly, then place in a serving bowl. Garnish with chopped coriander.

Serve with Rotli, your choice of rice and side dish.

If you are not serving the curry straight away, store it in the fridge in an airtight container for up to 3 days, then reheat until piping hot.

NOTE *To cook dal without a pressure cooker you will need to use a large, heavy-based saucepan with a tight-fitting lid and simmer until the lentils are tender. Since more steam is likely to escape from a regular pan, you will need to keep topping up with hot water. Timings and the amount of water required may vary but the lentils should be cooked until very soft.*

ROTLI, BHAAT, DAL
BREADS, RICE & DAL

ROTLI
CHAPATI
(V) (NF)

Rotli is one of the most common and traditional Indian breads, which is served with most curries. We eat with our fingers and normally break off a bit of the rotli and use it to scoop the curry up like a spoon. When cooking rotli, I have a separate gas burner on a high heat so once the rotli is cooked on the *tawa* (flat griddle), I place it directly over the naked flame for a few seconds. This makes the rotli puff up and then I stack and serve them. If you don't have a *tawa*, use a frying pan/skillet instead.

300 g/2¼ cups chapati atta (wholemeal/whole-wheat flour), plus extra for dusting
⅛ teaspoon salt
60 ml/¼ cup sunflower oil, plus extra for greasing
240 ml/1 cup lukewarm water
butter (optional if you prefer this to be vegan)

MAKES ABOUT 20 ROTLI

Sift the flour into a bowl, add the salt and oil and mix gently. Add the water, a little at a time, and gradually combine the ingredients. Use your hands to knead the dough until it becomes soft and pliable. If the dough is too sticky, add more flour and knead for several minutes. The dough should be smooth and when you press with your fingers, they should leave an impression.

Drizzle a small amount of oil to the palms of your hands and spread it over the dough. Cover the dough with a clean dish towel and leave to rest for 15 minutes.

Lightly dust a clean work surface with flour and place a *tawa* or frying pan/skillet over a low heat.

Take a piece of dough about 25 g/1 oz. in weight. Roll it into a ball between your palms and then press to flatten. Very lightly dust the dough on both sides with flour, shake to remove any excess and then roll into a 13–14-cm/5–5½-in. circle. If the dough is sticking to the work surface, add a little more flour to the surface.

Place the rotli on the hot *tawa* and once the sides start to bubble, flip the rotli and cook on the other side until small brown dots appear on the bottom.

On a separate gas burner over a high heat, use tongs to place the rotli over the naked flame and watch it puff up. Remove from the heat and place on a plate. Smear the rotli with a little butter on one side so the next rotli to be stacked on top doesn't stick to it. If you are vegan, skip this part and just place parchment paper on top of the cooked rotli.

Repeat until all the rotli have been cooked and stacked.

Wrap in kitchen foil to keep warm. Ideally, the rotli should be served warm, but they can be reheated for 1–2 minutes on each side if eaten later. Store any leftovers in an airtight container.

NOTE *Chapati atta or Indian wholemeal/whole-wheat flour is readily available in Asian shops and well-stocked supermarkets. If you can't get hold of it, mix equal quantities of wholemeal flour and plain/all-purpose flour.*

METHI NA DHEBRA
FENUGREEK & MILLET FLATBREAD
(V) (NF)

The millet flour gives this bread a rustic texture, which is a little thicker than other types of bread. I sometimes have Methi na Dhebra for breakfast with Keri no Chundo (see page 144). Yes, it sounds strange, but sometimes I quite like a savoury breakfast. However, dhebra can be eaten at any time, including at teatime.

Dried methi (fenugreek leaves) can be used, but nothing beats fresh methi. Be gentle when rolling as dough made with millet flour can be quite sticky. Once I roll the dough, I place the uncooked dhebra on a damp cloth, which I then use to transfer the bread to a hot frying pan/skillet. Just make sure to keep your cloth moist in between cooking each one.

100 g/3½ oz. methi
   (fresh fenugreek leaves)
25 g/1 oz. fresh coriander/
   cilantro, chopped
150 g/generous 1 cup millet flour
50 g/⅓ cup chapati atta
   (wholemeal/whole-wheat flour)
2 tablespoons sunflower oil,
   plus extra for frying
¾ teaspoon salt
⅛ teaspoon ground turmeric
½ tablespoon sesame seeds
1 teaspoon red chilli/chile powder
1 teaspoon carom seeds
1 tablespoon Ginger, Garlic and
   Chilli Paste (see page 14)
1 tablespoon granulated sugar
1 tablespoon fresh lemon juice
⅓ teaspoon asafoetida

TO SERVE
plant-based yogurt
pinch of red chilli/chili powder
pinch of cumin seeds

MAKES 10 DHEBRA

Mix all the ingredients together in a bowl and add 180 ml/⅔ cup water, a little at a time, and mix to combine. Knead the dough until smooth and it comes away easily from the bowl.

Place a 20-cm/8-in. square damp muslin cloth on a work surface.

Heat a drizzle of oil in a *tawa* or frying pan/skillet over a medium heat for 3 minutes.

Take a piece of dough about 50 g/1¾ oz. in weight. Roll the dough into a 13-cm/5-in. circle and place on the damp cloth. Lift the cloth and then flip the flatbread into the frying pan, peeling away the cloth.

After 20 seconds, add a drizzle of oil around the outside of the dhebra and use a spatula to lift the edges. After 30–40 seconds, flip the dhebra and fry on the other side for 1 minute. Add another drizzle of oil and flip again. Keep on frying and flipping for 2–3 minutes until the dhebra are brown on both sides, adding more oil as needed. Once cooked, transfer to a plate.

Wet the cloth with water and repeat until all the dough has been used, stacking the dhebra on top of each other. Keep them warm while you cook all the breads.

Serve the dhebra with yogurt and a pinch each of red chilli powder and cumin seeds.

TIP *This bread is popular for taking on long journeys as it keeps well for 2–3 days.*

MAKING DHEBRA

After picking methi (fenugreek) leaves from their stalks and making the dough mix in a bowl, I flatten the piece of dough on the stone/damp cloth and then roll out the dhebra using a *velan* (an Indian rolling pin used to roll bread). A normal rolling pin will also work fine.

ALOO PARATHA
SPICY POTATO STUFFED FLATBREAD
(V) (NF)

Aloo Paratha is a delicious flatbread stuffed with a spicy potato filling and pan fried. It makes a great breakfast or snack. There are various stages to this recipe – making the dough, making the spicy filling, stuffing the paratha, then pan-frying the paratha.

PARATHA DOUGH
250 g/9 oz. chapati atta (wholemeal/whole-wheat flour), plus extra for dusting
pinch of salt
2½ tablespoons sunflower oil, plus extra for drizzling
110 ml/scant ½ cup lukewarm water (this may vary according to the flour)

PARATHA FILLING
500 g/1 lb. 2 oz. boiled potatoes (boiled in their skins, then peeled)
1 teaspoon salt
40 g/2½ tablespoons granulated sugar
1 teaspoon fresh lemon juice
20 g/¾ oz. fresh coriander/cilantro
½ tablespoon garam masala
2 tablespoons Ginger, Garlic and Chilli Paste (see page 14)

TO SERVE
Limbu nu Athanu (see page 148, optional)

MAKES 12 PARATHA

First, make the dough. Sift the flour into a bowl, add the salt and oil and mix gently. Add the water, a little at a time, and gradually combine the ingredients. Use your hands to knead the dough until it becomes firm.

Drizzle a small amount of sunflower oil on the dough and use your hands to spread the oil over the dough. Cover with a clean dish cloth and leave to rest for 15 minutes. Remove the cloth and divide the dough into 12 equal-sized balls.

To make the filling, grate/shred the boiled potatoes into a bowl and add all the other filling ingredients. Use your hands to mix everything together gently. Make 12 equal-sized balls from the potato mixture and place on a plate.

Lightly dust a work surface with flour. Place a dough ball on the surface and gently press down with your fingers. Press the dough outwards, stretching the dough into a 8–10-cm/3–4-in. circle.

Place one of the potato balls in the middle of the dough and gently pull it upwards, wrapping it around the potato stuffing until it is completely covered. Remove any excess dough.

Place a *tawa* or frying pan/skillet over a low heat for 2 minutes.

Meanwhile, put the wrapped potato ball on the work surface and lightly sprinkle a little flour onto the ball. Very gently, roll the ball into a 12-cm/5-in. circle. Don't worry too much about the size, just make sure the paratha is not rolled too thin.

Place the paratha in the hot pan and dry-fry on one side for 20 seconds. Flip the paratha over and add a small drizzle of oil over the bread. Flip over again and add another small drizzle of oil to this side. Fry the paratha for 1 minute, occasionally pressing down with a spatula. Flip and fry the other side, pressing down again. Once the paratha is golden brown, it is ready. You may need to keep on flipping to make sure you don't burn the paratha.

Stuff and fry each paratha one at a time. Don't try stuffing and frying all the paratha in one go as they will become too soft and break apart.

Once the paratha are ready, serve with Limbu nu Athanu or just on their own.

PURI
PUFFED BREAD

Puri is a very popular puffy Indian bread made with just wheat flour, salt, oil and water. The dough is rolled into discs and deep-fried to make golden bread that tastes equally amazing with savoury curries or sweet dishes. Puri can be eaten with any curry, especially Bateta nu Shaak (see page 65). Puri with Masala Chai (see page 164) also makes a great breakfast, which I sometimes have when I'm not working. Just make sure you knead the dough harder than you would for a chapati and ensure that the oil is very hot before you begin frying. Puri is often served on happy occasions, such as weddings and festivals.

200 g/1½ cups chapati atta (wholemeal/whole-wheat flour), plus extra for dusting
⅛ teaspoon salt
2 teaspoons sunflower oil, plus extra for drizzling and deep-frying
75 ml/⅓ cup lukewarm water
Limbu nu Athanu (see page 148), to serve

MAKES 15 PURI

Sift the flour and salt into a bowl. Add the oil and combine gently. Add the water, a little at a time – how much you need will vary depending on the flour you are using. Knead the dough for a few minutes until it becomes firm and smooth, but not sticky.

Lightly drizzle oil over the dough, cover with a clean dish towel and leave to rest for 15 minutes.

Divide the dough into about 15 equal-sized pieces and roll each piece into a ball in the palm of your hands.

Lightly dust a work surface with flour. Place a dough ball on the surface and gently roll away from you using a rolling pin. Pick up the dough with your fingers and turn it 90 degrees, then roll again. Roll the puri into a 10–12-cm/4–5-in. disc. Don't worry too much if they are not perfectly round. Place the dough disc on a plate.

Repeat until all the puri have been rolled. Each time, place the rolled puri on a plate, but make sure they do not touch each other.

Heat enough oil for deep-frying in a heavy-based pan or wok over a medium heat. Check if the oil is hot enough by dropping a small piece of dough into the oil; if the dough rises, the oil is ready.

Gently lower the rolled puri into the hot oil and fry until it puffs up. Carefully turn the puri over and fry until golden brown. Once you have got the hang of this, you can cook several puri at the same time.

Remove the puri from the oil with a slotted spoon and place on kitchen paper to drain. Repeat until all the puri have been fried.

Serve hot or cold.

THIKKA THEPLA
TURMERIC & CHILLI FLATBREAD
(V) (NF)

This is our most popular bread served in the restaurant! Thepla are a lightly spiced flatbreads made from wheat flour and some simple spices. To make thepla, the dough should be quite soft and then fried gently on a hot *tawa* or frying pan/skillet. During cooking, lightly drizzle the thepla with oil to achieve those little brown spots over the surface. This ensures that the flatbreads remain soft. Thepla are amazing with any curry, but they're also great as a snack with Masala Chai (see page 164). I sometimes enjoy thepla with Limbu nu Athanu (see page 148) as a quick snack.

200 g/1½ cups chapati atta (wholemeal/whole-wheat flour), plus extra for dusting
½ teaspoon salt
¼ teaspoon ground turmeric
½ teaspoon carom seeds
½ teaspoon red chilli/chile powder
2 tablespoons sunflower oil, plus extra for drizzling

MAKES 10 THEPLA

Combine all the dry ingredients in a bowl and stir well. Add the oil and knead the dough. Add 100 ml/scant ½ cup water, a little at a time, until the dough comes together and is smooth, but not sticky. The dough is ready when you press with your finger and it springs back up.

Lightly drizzle oil over the dough, cover with a clean dish towel and leave to rest for about 20 minutes.

Divide the dough into about 10 equal-sized pieces and roll each piece into a ball in the palm of your hands.

Lightly dust a work surface, with flour. Place a dough ball on the surface, press down and gently roll away from you using a rolling pin. Pick up the dough with your fingers and turn it 90 degrees, then roll again. Roll the thepla into a 13–14-cm/5–5½-in. disc, which is neither too thin nor too thick. Place the dough disc on a plate. Repeat until all the thepla have been rolled, placing parchment paper between each one as you stack them.

Place a *tawa* or frying pan/skillet over a low heat for a couple of minutes. Place the thepla onto the hot *tawa* and cook on one side for 1 minute or until small bubbles appear on the edges. Flip the thepla over using a spatula and fry on the other side until bubbles appear again.

Lightly drizzle a little oil around the edges of the thepla. Use the spatula, press down to stop the thepla puffing up. Flip the thepla over, add another drizzle of oil around the edges again and remove the thepla to a plate. Repeat until all the thepla have been cooked.

BHAAT
RICE
(V) (GF) (NF)

There are limitless recipes for cooking rice, some very complicated, others not so. This method is as easy as it gets and is how we cook rice in the restaurant. Rice is pretty much always served with a main Gujarati meal.

250 g/scant 1½ cups basmati rice
¾ teaspoon salt
½ teaspoon sunflower oil

SERVES 4

Place the rice in a large bowl. Cover with lukewarm water and wash thoroughly. Repeat until the water remains clear – you may need to do this 6 or 7 times. It's important to wash the rice thoroughly to remove as much starch as possible. Cover the washed rice with fresh water and leave to soak for at least 15 minutes.

Pour 1 litre/4 cups water into a wide pan and place over a high heat. Add the salt and oil and bring the water to the boil. Add the rice to the pan and cook, uncovered, for about 8 minutes. Check if the rice is cooked by squeezing a few grains in between your fingers; if it crushes, the rice is cooked. We prefer the grains to be slightly firm, but if you like the rice softer just cook it for a little longer.

Drain the rice and serve.

KHICHDI
SIMPLE RICE LENTIL DISH
(V) (GF) (NF)

Khichdi is a comfort food believed to have healing powers, so it's often given to the sick. It's also one of the first solids Indian babies eat as it is easy to digest. Serve with Khadi (see page 100) or Chaas (see page 167).

100 g/generous ½ cup tuvar dal (yellow lentils/dried pigeon peas)
300 g/1⅔ cups basmati rice
½ tablespoon salt
½ teaspoon ground turmeric
3 x 3-cm/1¼-in. cinnamon sticks
5–6 cloves
1 tablepoon ghee (or sunflower oil if you prefer this to be vegan)

SERVES 4

Place the dal in a bowl. Cover with water and wash thoroughly. Repeat 5 or 6 times. Cover the washed dal with fresh water and leave to soak for 15 minutes. Wash the rice until the water runs clear, then soak in a bowl of cold water for 15 minutes. Make sure the dal and rice are fully submerged in water.

Pour 2.5 litres/quarts water into a large pan with a lid. Cover with a lid, place over a high heat and bring the water to the boil. Add the salt, turmeric, cinnamon sticks, cloves and ghee or oil.

Drain the dal and add to the pan. Cover and boil for 15 minutes or until the dal is ready. Check by squeezing a piece of dal between your finger and thumb; it should crush easily. Cooking times for dal vary, so adjust accordingly.

Drain the rice and add to the dal in the pan. Cover and cook for 10 minutes. Turn off the heat and leave to rest, uncovered, for a few minutes.

MATAR BHAAT
VEGETABLE RICE
(V) (GF)

150 g/¾ cup basmati rice
1 tablespoon ghee (or sunflower
   oil if you prefer this to be vegan)
1 teaspoon cumin seeds
3 bay leaves
3 cloves
3 x 4-cm/1½-in. cinnamon sticks
1 carrot, peeled and diced
1 potato, peeled and diced
40 g/⅓ cup fresh peas (defrosted
   if using frozen)
1 teaspoon salt
pinch of ground turmeric
10–12 sultanas/golden raisins
15 cashew nuts

SERVES 4

Matar bhaat is a traditional rice dish made with spices, carrots and of course, peas. I also add cashews and sultanas/golden raisins. This is lovely served with Khadi (see below).

Wash the rice until the water runs clear and then soak in a bowl of fresh cold water for 15 minutes.

Place a saucepan over a medium heat and add the ghee or oil. Once the ghee has melted, add the cumin seeds. Once they start to crackle, add the bay leaves, cloves and cinnamon sticks and stir quickly to combine.

Add the carrot, potato and peas and cook for 2 minutes.

Add 600 ml/2½ cups water and bring to the boil. Add the rice and remaining ingredients to the pan. Stir gently a couple of times, cover the pan with a lid and then leave it for 10 minutes. After 10 minutes, check if the rice is cooked. If the rice is still not cooked, add 2 tablespoons water and cook uncovered until the rice is ready.

This rice can be stored in the fridge for 2–3 days.

KHADI
GRAM FLOUR & YOGURT SOUP
(GF) (NF)

170 g/¾ cup plain yogurt
   (don't use thick/set yogurt)
30 g/¼ cup chickpea/gram flour
1 teaspoon salt
1 teaspoon granulated sugar
1½ tablespoons Ginger and Garlic
   Paste (see page 14)
1 green chilli/chili, crushed
handful of chopped fresh
   coriander/cilantro, to garnish

VAGAR (TEMPERED OIL)
2 teaspoons ghee (or oil)
1 dried red chilli/chili
½ teaspoon cumin seeds
¼ teaspoon fenugreek seeds
3 cloves
12–15 curry leaves
¼ teaspoon asafoetida

SERVES 2

Khadi is a Gujarati spiced yogurt soup, thickened using chickpea/gram flour. It's sweet, sour and spicy in taste. It makes great comfort food during cold evenings and is best served with plain rice or Matar Bhaat (see above).

Place the yogurt, chickpea flour, salt, sugar, ginger and garlic paste and green chilli in a wide bowl. Mix together and slowly add 500 ml/2 cups water, mixing as you go. Use a balloon whisk to make sure the mixture is smooth and free from any lumps.

Place a large pan over a medium heat and add the ghee or oil. Once the ghee has melted, add the dried red chilli. Fry for 30–40 seconds and then add the cumin seeds.

Once they start to crackle, add the rest of the ingredients and stir quickly to combine.

Add the yogurt mixture to the hot ghee or oil and stir to mix.

Reduce the heat to low and simmer for 12–15 minutes, stirring continuously to make sure the yogurt doesn't split. If the mixture becomes too thick, add a little water to loosen.

Remove from the heat and add the coriander to garnish.

GUJARATI DAL
LENTIL SOUP
(V) (GF) (NF)

This Gujarati dal is one of my favourites and I make it at least once a week. Don't be put off by the number of ingredients needed, they make a wonderfully fragrant soup. Give it a go as Gujarati dal is very different to other dals. This dal has two contrasting flavours – sweet and sour. The sweetness comes from the palm sugar/jaggery and the sourness comes from *kokum* (a dried fruit from the Goan butter tree). If you struggle to find *kokum*, use tamarind paste instead and adjust to taste accordingly. This dal is delicious with any curry, rice and Rotli (see page 86).

100 g/½ cup tuvar dal (yellow lentils/dried pigeon peas)
480 ml/2 cups boiling water
⅛ teaspoon ground turmeric
⅛ teaspoon salt
handful of chopped fresh coriander/cilantro, to garnish

MASALA MIX
1 piece of kokum (dried fruit from Goan butter tree)
3-cm/1¼-in. piece of fresh ginger, peeled and chopped
⅛ teaspoon ground turmeric
½ teaspoon red chilli/chile powder
½ teaspoon ground coriander
½ teaspoon garam masala
½ teaspoon salt
½ tablespoon granulated sugar
½ tablespoon palm sugar/jaggery
120 ml/½ cup canned chopped tomatoes
2 tablespoons tomato ketchup
1 green chilli/chili, halved lengthwise

VAGAR (TEMPERED OIL)
2 tablespoons sunflower oil
1 dried red chilli/chili
2 cloves
½ teaspoon mustard seeds
⅓ teaspoon fenugreek seeds
¼ teaspoon asafoetida

SERVES 4

First, make the masala mix. Place the kokum in a small dish and add a drizzle of water. Squash and squeeze the kokum, then transfer to a bowl. Add all the remaining ingredients for the masala mix to the bowl, combine well and set aside.

Place the dal in a bowl and wash in lukewarm water. Drain and repeat several times until the water remains clear. Place the washed dal in a saucepan, pour over the boiling water, leave to soak for 30 minutes and then drain.

Place a separate large saucepan over a high heat, add 720 ml/3 cups water, the soaked dal, turmeric and salt. Bring to the boil, then simmer over a medium heat for 30 minutes. Use a metal spoon to skim off any foam that forms on the surface of the water. Check the dal is ready by squeezing a piece in between your thumb and finger; the dal should crush easily, otherwise carry on simmering.

Remove from the heat and use a handheld blender to blend the dal to your preference, either totally smooth or with more texture. Return the dal to the heat.

Next, make the vagar. Heat the oil in a small saucepan set over a medium heat for 90 seconds. Check the oil is hot enough by adding a few mustard seeds; if they sizzle the oil is ready. Combine the dried chilli, cloves, mustard seeds, fenugreek seeds and asafoetida in a small bowl, then add to the hot oil. Heat for 2 minutes, stirring continuously.

Add the vagar and masala mix to the dal, stir together and add 360 ml/1½ cups water. Turn up the heat to high and cook, stirring continuously, for 5–6 minutes. Remove from the heat and garnish with the coriander.

NASTO
SNACKS

JADI SEV
THICK CHICKPEA & PEPPER NOODLES
(V) (GF) (NF)

These are a deliciously moreish snack. They're eaten during Diwali, however, I enjoy these all year round too. Made from chickpea/gram flour and spices – I particularly love the black pepper in these noodles – the medium-thick, crispy strands are extruded by a sancha machine (see page 114) and then deep-fried. This snack goes perfectly with Masala Chai (see page 164).

250 g/1¾ cups chickpea/gram
    flour
1 teaspoon salt
1 teaspoon carom seeds
¼ teaspoon ground turmeric
1 teaspoon red chilli/chile powder
1 teaspoon black peppercorns
sunflower oil, for deep-frying

sancha machine, with medium hole plate attached, greased lightly with sunflower oil

SERVES 4

Sift the flour into a bowl to remove any lumps. Use the back of a spoon to press through any large lumps of flour. This is an important step to achieve the correct texture for sev. Add the salt, carom seeds, turmeric and red chilli powder to the flour.

Use a pestle and mortar to crush the black peppercorns to a fine powder and add to the flour. Use your hands to slowly mix together all the ingredients.

Make a well in the middle of the flour. Slowly add 120 ml/½ cup water, a little at a time, and mix it into the flour. Continue mixing the batter in a circular motion until it has a soft, smooth texture.

Place a heavy-based frying pan/skillet over a medium heat and add enough sunflower oil for deep-frying.

Add a drizzle of oil to the sancha machine and lightly grease the chamber and top of the machine. Add the batter to the chamber of the sancha machine, keeping a tiny bit of dough aside.

Check if the oil is hot enough by placing the reserved small piece of dough into the oil; if it rises, the oil is ready.

Starting at the edge of the pan furthest away from you, turn the handle of the sancha machine so sev strands start to fall into the hot oil. Move the sancha around the perimeter of the pan, while turning the handle, to complete the circle. Once you get back to the starting point, move inwards, without stopping, and complete another circle around the pan.

Fry the sev for 15 seconds, then push the strands down into the oil slightly. Now, using a fork in each hand, slowly lift the sev upwards and out of the oil, then gently drop them back again. This stops the sev sticking together and ensures they cook evenly.

Once the sev reach a golden-brown colour, lift them out of the oil, turn and then fry on the other side until golden brown, gently pushing the sev down into the oil every so often.

Once the sev are ready, remove them from the oil and place on kitchen paper to drain. Repeat until all the sev have been fried, stacking them on top of each other. Leave to cool.

The sev can be stored in an airtight container for up to 6 months.

SEV

THIN CHICKPEA NOODLES

(V) (GF) (NF)

Sev are crispy noodles made from chickpea/gram flour, which are eaten by themselves as well as being widely used in Indian street-food dishes, such as Sev Mamra (see opposite). This recipe does require a sancha machine, a noodle extruder with a metal chamber that has different plates used to make various Indian snacks. Use the smallest plate possible here. A smooth dough is added to the sancha and pressed into thin strands or noodles that are dropped into hot oil, which fries them into a crunchy snack.

250 g/1¾ cups chickpea/gram flour
1 teaspoon salt
¼ teaspoon ground turmeric
sunflower oil, for deep-frying

sancha machine, with small hole plate attached, greased lightly with sunflower oil

SERVES 4

Sift the flour into a bowl to remove any lumps. Use the back of a spoon to press through any large lumps of flour. This is an important step to achieve the correct texture for sev. Add the salt and turmeric to the flour. Use your hands to slowly mix together all the ingredients.

Make a well in the middle of the flour. Slowly add 120 ml/½ cup water, a little at a time, and mix it into the flour. Knead the dough for about 10 minutes, or until it has a soft, smooth texture. The dough should be neither too soft, nor too hard.

Place a heavy-based frying pan/skillet over a medium heat and add enough sunflower oil for deep-frying. Add a drizzle of oil to the sancha machine and lightly grease the chamber and top of the machine. Add the batter to the chamber of the sancha machine, keeping a tiny bit of dough aside.

Check if the oil is hot enough by placing the reserved small piece of dough into the oil; if it rises, the oil is ready.

Starting at the edge of the pan furthest away from you, turn the handle of the sancha machine so sev strands start to fall into the hot oil. Move the sancha around the perimeter of the pan, while turning the handle, to complete the circle. Once you get back to the starting point, move inwards, without stopping, and complete another circle around the pan.

Fry the sev for 15 seconds, then push the strands down into the oil slightly. Now, using a fork in each hand, slowly lift the sev upwards and out of the oil, then gently drop them back down again. This stops the sev sticking together and ensures they cook evenly.

Once the sev reach a golden-brown colour, lift them out of the oil, turn and then fry on the other side until golden brown, gently pushing the sev down into the oil every so often.

Remove the sev from the oil and place on kitchen paper to drain. Repeat until all the sev have been fried, stacking them on top of each other. Leave to cool completely.

Enjoy the sev on its own or use it as part of other dishes. The sev can be stored in an airtight container for up to 6 months.

SEV MAMRA
PUFFED RICE & CRISPY NOODLES
(V) (GF)

A great snack made using puffed rice and crispy noodles, which is high up in the deliciousness department. Basically, there are two main parts. The *sev* (thin chickpea noodles) and *mamra* (puffed rice) are combined with spices to create a crunchy snack that is both savoury and sweet. I usually make this in large batches, which doesn't really require much more effort. Sev mamra is great as a snack at tea-time or on the go. It's also a key ingredient in Bhel (see page 129) and delicious enjoyed with Masala Chai (see page 164)

500 g/1 lb. 2 oz. puffed rice
200 g/1½ cups peanuts
60 ml/¼ cup sunflower oil
1 tablespoon cumin seeds
½ teaspoon asafoetida
15–20 curry leaves
1 teaspoon ground turmeric
2 teaspoons red chilli/chile powder
2 teaspoons salt
2 tablespoons icing/ confectioners' sugar
200 g/7 oz. Sev (see opposite)

MAKES ABOUT 950 G/2 LB.

Place a very large pan over a medium heat. After 2 minutes, add the puffed rice to the dry pan and cook, stirring continuously, to stop the puffed rice from catching on the bottom of the pan. Continue stirring until the rice turns a light golden colour and crispy. Turn off the heat and leave the puffed rice to cool.

Heat the oil in a frying pan/skillet over a high heat for 2–3 minutes. Add the peanuts, reduce the heat to low and gently fry the nuts, stirring occasionally, for about 2–3 minutes until they turn a dark brown colour. Remove the peanuts from the oil and spread them out on a clean dish towel to cool.

To the same pan and oil, add the cumin seeds and once they start to crackle, add the asafoetida, curry leaves, turmeric, then immediately add them to the puffed rice. Stir together, then add the chilli powder, salt and peanuts.

Place a sieve/strainer over the puffed rice and put the icing sugar into the sieve. Shake to sift the icing sugar over the rice.

Add the sev to the pan and use both hands to gently combine all the ingredients. Leave to cool completely.

The sev mamra can be stored in an airtight container for up to 3 months.

NOTE *Puffed rice can easily be bought but sometimes I dehydrate cooked rice and store it in a jar ready to use. It's easy to do, just spread cooked rice on a tray and place near a radiator. The dehydrated rice becomes very hard, which I fry before using in this recipe.*

CHAKRI
SAVOURY CRISPY SWIRLS

This spiral-shaped savoury snack – crispy, crunchy and hugely popular in India – is made using rice flour, potato and spices. To make the spirals, you will need a sancha machine – a tall, cylindrical extruder with a long rotating handle and shaped plates – which is used to create different Indian snacks. They are available to buy online and at larger Asian grocery stores.

100 g/¾ cup rice flour
70 g/2¾ oz. mashed potato (potatoes boiled with skins on, then peeled and mashed)
1 tablespoon melted butter
1 teaspoon salt
pinch of carom seeds
1 teaspoon sesame seeds
2 tablespoons Ginger and Garlic Paste (see page 14)
25 g/1 oz. semolina
sunflower oil, for deep-frying

sancha machine, with star-shaped plate, greased lightly with sunflower oil

MAKES ABOUT 20 CHAKRI

Place the rice flour, mashed potato, butter, salt, carom seeds, sesame seeds and ginger and garlic paste in a mixing bowl and mix until everything is combined. Set aside.

Place a saucepan over a low heat, then add the semolina. Dry roast, shaking the pan every so often, for just a few minutes or until the semolina is golden brown. Add 70 ml/generous ¼ cup water and stir continuously until all the water has been absorbed by the semolina – a little bit of water left behind is fine. Remove the pan from the heat and leave to cool.

Once the semolina is cool to the touch, add it to the bowl with the other ingredients. Slowly combine and knead the dough for 1 minute. The dough should still be quite rough. Cover with a clean dish towel and leave to rest for 30 minutes.

Add a drizzle of oil to the sancha machine and lightly grease the chamber and top of the machine. Wet your hands, give the dough a quick massage, then gently place the dough inside the sancha. Firmly close the lid.

On a clean work surface, make the chakri spirals by starting from the centre and slowly working outwards. Don't get too caught up in achieving the perfect spiral,

they'll taste great no matter what shape they are. Each spiral should be around 6–7 cm/2½–3 in. in diameter. Again, it doesn't really matter what size they are. Break the length of dough from the sancha and press the end of the dough into the sides of the chakri to finish the spiral. This is an important step as it stops the chakri from breaking when frying.

Place a heavy-based pan over a medium heat and add enough sunflower oil for deep-frying. Check the oil is hot enough by placing a small piece of dough into the oil; if it rises, the oil is ready.

Turn the heat to low. Use a spatula (not your hands) to carefully lift a chakri from the work surface and slowly lower it into the hot oil. Only fry a few chakri at a time, otherwise they will break in the pan. Fry the chakri for a few minutes on each side until they reach a light golden colour, then gently flip them over and fry on the other side. Once both sides are evenly golden, remove the chakri from the oil and place on kitchen paper to drain. Leave to cool completely. They will become crispy as they cool.

The chakri can be stored in an airtight container for up to 6 weeks.

GATHIYA
GUJARATI SAVOURY STRANDS
(V) (GF) (NF)

Gathiya is an incredibly popular and much-loved snack in Gujarat. While the preparation of the batter may take some time, frying the gathiya is quick and easy, just make sure the batter is soft and smooth before you fry it. Due to busy lifestyles, I'm finding more and more people are turning to shop-bought snacks instead of making them at home, but this is well worth the effort! These thick noodles can be eaten any time of the day, including breakfast. They are delicious served with Lili Chutney (see page 147), Sambharo (see page 139) and Masala Chai (see page 164).

500 g/3¾ cups chickpea/gram flour
½ teaspoon carom seeds
2 teaspoons black peppercorns, crushed in a pestle and mortar
1 teaspoon salt
2 teaspoons bicarbonate of soda (baking soda)
120 ml/½ cup sunflower oil, plus extra for deep-frying
¼ teaspoon asafoetida

gathiya jaro (a flat metal utensil similiar to a frying pan/skillet with lots of small star-shaped holes in it) or a sancha machine

MAKES ABOUT 600 G/1 LB. 5 OZ.

Sift the flour into a bowl to remove any lumps. Use the back of a spoon to press through any large lumps of flour. Add the carom seeds and crushed black pepper, stir through the flour and set aside.

Place a saucepan over a low heat, then add the salt and bicarbonate of soda. Dry roast for 3 minutes, using a spatula to stir continuously, then remove the pan from the heat.

Slowly and carefully add 240 ml/1 cup cold water to the pan – the mixture will spit once the water is added, so do this over a sink. Mix together and set aside to cool for a couple of minutes.

Add the oil and asafoetida to the pan and use a handheld blender to whisk for 30 seconds until the mixture starts to foam.

Add the blended mixture to the bowl with the flour and slowly start to combine. Work the mixture until the dough is soft, smooth and free from any lumps.

Place a large, wide pan over a low heat and add enough sunflower oil for deep-frying.

Check if the oil is hot enough by placing a tiny piece of dough into the oil; if it rises, the oil is ready.

Rest the jaro on top of the pan above the hot oil. Give the dough a quick knead, then place a large ball of the dough on top of the jaro. Push the dough through the holes of the jaro so the strands fall into the hot oil below. Use the heel of your hand and work with long, back-and-forth motions to ensure your gathiya are long in length.

Gently fry the gathiya for about 3–4 minutes, flipping them over with a slotted spoon every so often, until they are evenly cooked and very lightly golden. Remove the gathiya from the oil and place on kitchen paper to drain.

Remove the jaro from the hot pan, wet it with cold water and place it back on the pan over the oil. Repeat until all the gathiya have been fried. Leave to cool completely.

The gathiya can be stored in an airtight container for up to 3–4 months.

MAKING GATHIYA

I use a jaro to shape gathiya. A jaro is a flat metal utensil, similar to a frying pan/skillet, but with lots of star-shaped holes in the bottom. The gathiya dough is pushed through the holes in the jaro to create the strand shapes of this popular snack, which then drop into the hot oil below to be deep-fried. You could achieve the same affect with a colander.

FARSI PURI
DEEP-FRIED CRISPY FLATBREAD
(V) (NF)

Farsi Puri are crispy, flaky fried breads. Guajaratis love these and every household will have a container full during Diwali. When we sold snacks via our website, these were on the menu and people loved them! Enjoy as a snack with Masala Chai (see page 164).

200 g/1½ cups plain/all-purpose flour
1 teaspoon freshly ground black pepper
½ teaspoon salt
½ teaspoon brown or white sesame seeds
50 ml/3½ tablespoons melted butter (or use sunflower oil if you prefer these to be vegan)

MAKES ABOUT 20 PURI

Place the flour, black pepper, salt and sesame seeds in a bowl and mix together. Add the melted butter and gently knead into a dough. Gradually add 50 ml/¼ cup water, a little at a time, and knead until the dough becomes smooth but firm. Cover with a clean dish towel and leave to rest for 30 minutes.

Wet your hands and knead the dough for 30 seconds – it should still be quite firm. Divide the dough into 20 equal-sized balls, each about 15 g/½ oz. in weight.

On a clean work surface, add a drizzle of oil and roll the balls into 10-cm/4-in. circles. Use a knife to make 7 or 8 small slits in the puri – this stops the puri puffing up during frying. Place on a plate ready to fry.

Place a heavy-based pan over a high heat and add enough sunflower oil for deep-frying. Check if the oil is ready by placing a small piece of dough into the oil; if it rises, the oil is ready. Lower the heat to medium.

Lower a few puri into the hot oil. They will slowly rise to the surface. Push the puri down into the oil and fry for 1 minute. Flip the puri over and fry on the other side for 1 minute, pushing each puri down into the oil and then flip again. Continue doing this until the puri reach a light golden brown colour. Remove the puri from the oil and place on kitchen paper to drain.

The puri can be stored in an airtight container for up to 6 months.

NOTES *If you want to make these vegan, replace the melted butter with sunflower oil; just make sure the dough reaches the right consistency.*

Use this recipe to make Papdi Chaat (see page 126), just roll the puri smaller than instructed in this recipe to around 5 cm/2 in. each.

CHAAT
STREET FOOD

MASALA MISRANA
STREET-FOOD MASALA MIX
(V) (GF) (NF)

Most Gujarati street-food dishes use a masala chickpea/garbanzo bean and potato base. I make this simple base recipe for my chaat dishes in advance, as well as various chutneys, and assemble everything just before serving.

1 large potato
200 g/1¼ cups canned
    chickpeas/garbanzo beans
¼ teaspoon red chilli/chile
    powder
½ teaspoon salt
½ teaspoon chaat masala
½ teaspoon ground coriander
1 teaspoon ground cumin
½ teaspoon fresh lemon juice

MAKES ABOUT 250 G/1½ CUPS

Boil the unpeeled potato in a saucepan of salted water for about 10 minutes or until tender. Remove the potato from the pan, leave to cool and then peel away the skin.

Cut the potato into small cubes (don't worry too much about the shape and size) and put into a bowl. Add all the remaining ingredients and mix well.

The masala mix can be stored in an airtight container in the fridge for up to 3 days. Use as instructed in the snack recipes in this chapter.

PANI PURI
PUFFED PURI FILLED WITH
MASALA MIX & TAMARIND WATER
(V) (NF)

This is one of India's most famous street-food dishes, which is eaten throughout the country. The best street-food vendors have long queues. If you are in India and want to eat pani puri, always join the longest line.

5 tablespoons Amli Chutney
    (see page 147)
16 shop-bought puri
60 g/2¾ oz. Masala Misrana
    (see above)
handful of Sev (see page 110)
chopped fresh coriander/
    cilantro or micro leaf coriander,
    to garnish
pomegranate seeds, to garnish

SERVES 4

To make *pani* (tamarind water), place 2 tablespoons of the Amli Chutney in a bowl and stir in 4 tablespoons water. Set aside.

Carefully remove part of the top of each puri to make a hole. Fill each puri with some of the Masala Misrana, followed by a dollop of the remaining Amli Chutney. Scatter a pinch of Sev into each puri, then garnish with chopped coriander and pomegranate seeds.

When ready to eat, pour some of the reserved *pani* (tamarind water) into the puri and pop the whole thing in your mouth in one go.

NOTE *This street food is also known as* gol gapa, puchka *and* pakoda.
We always use shop-bought puri for this recipe as they need to be crispy to hold the filling.

SAMOSA CHAAT
SAMOSA CHICKPEA & CHUTNEY CHAAT

8 Samosa (see page 42), broken into large pieces
8 tablespoons Masala Misrana (see page 122)
8 Farsi Puri (see page 118), broken into pieces
4 tablespoons Amli Chutney (see page 147)
4 tablespoons Lal Chutney (see page 140)
2 tablespoons Lili Chutney (see page 147)
4 tablespoons Mithu Dahi (see page 136)
handful of Sev (see page 110)
handful of chopped fresh coriander/cilantro
handful of pomegranate seeds

SERVES 4

This street-style chaat is a flavour bomb. It's the perfect dish to serve at a party because the different elements can be prepared ahead, then simply assembled and served cold. At Manju's we serve samosa chaat in a martini glass so all the various layers of chutneys can be seen. It is our most-photographed dish!

Divide the samosa pieces between four Martini glasses or shallow bowls. Add 2 tablespoons of the Masala Misrana to each bowl or glass, then top with the farsi puri pieces.

Drizzle 1 tablespoon of each of the three chutneys and the Mithu Dahi into each bowl or glass, making the dish look as colourful as possible.

Scatter the sev evenly over each bowl or glass, then garnish with chopped coriander and pomegranate seeds.

Eat straight away while the puri and samosa pastry are crispy; if left too long, they will turn soft.

TIPS *If you have any pastry leftover from making the samosa (see page 42), deep-fry it until golden and then use it in this dish for some extra crunch.*

If you are using samosa that have been partially fried and frozen, just make sure they are defrosted and fried until piping hot before using in this dish.

PAPDI CHAAT
CRISPY CRACKER CHAAT

16 papdi (shop-bought or see Tip below)
6 tablespoons Masala Misrana (see page 122)
6 tablespoons Mithu Dahi (see page 136)
5 tablespoons Amli Chutney (see page 147)
4 tablespoons Lal Chutney (see page 140)
3 tablespoons Lili Chutney (see page 147)
handful of Sev (see page 110)
handful of fresh coriander/cilantro, leaves picked
handful of pomegranate seeds

SERVES 4

Papdi chaat is a very famous street food. The flavours are amazing – sweet, sour and spicy – and they make the perfect canapé due to the small size of the papdi.

Place the papdi on a large tray. Using a teaspoon, put a small amount of the Masala Misrana on each papdi, then ctop with a little of the Mithu Dahi.

Dot the papdi with a small dollop of each of the three chutneys, then scatter over a pinch of Sev. Finally, garnish with chopped coriander and pomegranate seeds.

Eat straight away while the puri are crispy; if left too long, they will turn soft.

TIP *If you are making the papdi rather than using shop-bought ones, follow the recipe for Farsi Puri (see page 118), however, roll each puri to 5 cm/2 in. instead of 10 cm/4 in.*

BHEL
PUFFED RICE, CHICKPEAS & CHUTNEY CHAAT
(V)

Although Bhel originated in Mumbai, it's much loved and eaten throughout India. There are many variations of this tangy, spicy and crispy dish, so just go with the flow and adjust according to your taste.

PANI (TAMARIND WATER)
8 tablespoons Amli Chutney
  (see page 147)

BHEL
100 g/3½ oz. Sev Mamra
  (see page 111)
12 tablespoons Masala Misrana
  (see page 122)
12 Farsi Puri (see page 118)
4 tablespoons Amli Chutney
  (see page 147)
4 tablespoons Lal Chutney
  (see page 140)
2 tablespoons Lili Chutney
  (see page 147)
handful of Sev (see page 110)
1 red onion, diced
2 red tomatoes, diced
1 small green (unripe) mango,
  peeled and diced
1 green chilli/chili, chopped
½ teaspoon chaat masala
  (optional)
handful of chopped fresh
  coriander/cilantro
handful of pomegranate seeds

SERVES 4

To make *pani* (tamarind water), place the Amli Chutney in a bowl and mix in 8 tablespoons water. Set aside.

Next, make the bhel. Combine the Sev Mamra and Masala Misrana in a bowl. Break the puri into the bowl, then add the tamarind water and all three of the chutneys. Stir well to mix everything thoroughly.

Divide the bhel between four bowls. Scatter over the Sev, red onion, tomatoes, mango and chilli.

Lightly sprinkle the chaat masala over each bowl, if using. Finally, garnish with chopped coriander and pomegranate seeds.

Eat straight away while the puri are crispy; if left too long, they will turn soft.

DAHI VADA
LENTIL FRITTERS COATED IN YOGURT
(GF) (NF)

This is a lovely dish to eat on a warm summer's day. Cooling *dahi* (yogurt) and *vada* (lentil fritters) are a perfect match. The soft, savoury, sweet Dahi Vada are a combination of all my favourite flavours and textures. The fritters are drenched in a creamy yogurt and topped with sweet and spicy chutneys to finish. Perfect as a starter to a main meal or lunch.

250 g/9 oz. urad dal (skinless)
2 green chillies/chilis
15 g/½ oz. piece of fresh ginger
1½ teaspoons salt, plus extra
   for the yogurt
sunflower oil, for deep-frying
600 g/2½ cups plain yogurt
2 tablespoons milk
Amli Chutney (see page 147)
Lili Chutney (see page 147)

TO SERVE
ground cumin
red chilli/chile powder
pomegranate seeds (optional)
chopped fresh coriander/cilantro

MAKES ABOUT 40 FRITTERS

Place the urad dhal in a large bowl and wash several times until the water remains clear.

Add 700 ml/3 cups cold water so the dhal is completely covered and leave to soak for at least 4 hours, but ideally overnight.

Drain the dal, discard the water and transfer to a blender. Add the chillies, ginger and salt and blend to a smooth paste. Add a splash of water, if required, but don't overdo it; the batter should be thick rather than runny. If you add too much water, just add a pinch of rice flour to thicken the batter.

Heat enough sunflower oil for deep-frying in a heavy-based pan over a medium heat. Check the oil is hot enough by adding a few drops of batter to the oil; if the batter rises, the oil is ready.

Take a tablespoon of batter and carefully drop it into the oil. Using a slotted spoon, move the vada gently in the oil, turning them over every so often, making sure they don't stick together in the oil. Cook for 3–4 minutes or until golden brown. Remove the vada and place on kitchen paper to drain.

Continue frying the vada in batches until the batter is used up.

Bring a saucepan of water to the boil. Turn off the heat, add the vada to the hot water and leave to soak for 30 minutes.

Remove the vada from the pan and gently squeeze each one to remove any excess water.

In a bowl, combine the yogurt and ⅛ teaspoon salt and whisk gently to mix.

Drizzle the milk over the base of a baking pan and arrange the vada in the pan. Pour the yogurt over the vada, covering them as much as possible, and add generous amounts of both chutneys on top.

Sprinkle over the cumin, chilli powder, pomegranate seeds, if using, and chopped coriander to garnish.

Serve cold. The dahi vada can be stored in the fridge for up to 2 days.

NOTE *This dish does require a bit of forward planning as the urad dal needs to be soaked. I soak the dal overnight, but it needs a minimum of at least 4 hours as urad dal is very firm.*

VADA PAV
POTATO FRITTERS IN A BUN WITH CHUTNEYS
(V)

The king of Indian street food! A quick grab-and-go burger, which is made in front of you on the side streets of India. A *vada* (spicy potato fritter) is sandwiched in between a *pav* (soft bun) along with chutneys! Fried *bhundi* (chickpea pearls) and green chilli are added, but these are optional extras.

NUT CHUTNEY
1¼ tablespoons unsalted, skinless peanuts
½ teaspoon sunflower oil
4 garlic cloves
small pinch of salt
1 tablespoon Kashmiri chilli/ chile powder

VADA
1 large potato
1 teaspoon salt
½ teaspoon red chilli/chile powder
1 teaspoon garam masala
1 teaspoon Ginger, Garlic and Chilli Paste (see page 14)
1½ tablespoons granulated sugar
1 tablespoon fresh lemon juice
handful of fresh coriander/ cilantro leaves

BATTER
50 g/⅓ cup chickpea/gram flour
2 tablespoons cornflour/ cornstarch
pinch of salt
¼ teaspoon fresh lemon juice
sunflower oil, for deep-frying

TO SERVE
4 green chillies/chilis, sliced in half lengthways if large
4 soft white bread rolls
4 teaspoons Lili Chutney (see page 147)
4 teaspoons Amli Chutney (see page 147)

SERVES 4

First, make the nut chutney. Lightly toast the peanuts in a dry frying pan/skillet over a low heat. Add the oil and garlic and cook for about 3–4 minutes or until golden. Remove the pan from the heat and leave to cool. Transfer the toasted nuts and garlic to a blender, add the salt and Kashmiri chilli powder and pulse briefly to coarsely chop the nuts. Set aside.

Make the vada. Boil the potato in its skin in a pan of salted water until soft, then remove and leave to cool. Once cool, peel away the skin and grate the potato into a bowl. Add all the remaining ingredients for the vada and mix, so everything is combined and the potato is mashed.

Add a few drops of oil to the palms of your hands, then roll the potato mixture into 4 equal-sized balls and place on a plate.

To make the batter, sift the chickpea flour and cornflour into a bowl. Add the salt and lemon juice and slowly start to combine by gradually adding water, a little at a time – you should only need about 60 ml/¼ cup. Continue mixing until the batter is smooth and free of any lumps. The batter should not be too runny but thick enough to coat a spoon. Set aside.

Heat enough oil for deep-frying in a wok or large frying pan/skillet over a high heat for 2 minutes. Check if the oil is hot enough by dropping a piece of batter into the oil; if it rises, the oil is ready.

Lower the heat to medium. Take a few vada and roll them in the batter, making sure the potato balls are completely coated. Shake off any excess batter and carefully lower the vada into the hot oil.

Using a slotted spoon, move the vada gently, turning them over every so often, making sure they don't stick together. Cook for 3–4 minutes or until golden brown. Remove the vada from the oil and place on kitchen paper to drain. Continue cooking the vada in batches until all the potato balls are used.

To make *bhundi*, hold a colander/strainer over the hot oil and push any remaining batter through the holes using a spoon. Fry the droplets of batter, stirring occasionally, until golden. Remove and set aside.

Fry the green chillies in the oil for 1 minute. Remove and set aside.

Now, assemble the vada pav. Slice three-quarters of the way through each roll, making sure not to cut all the way. Spread a teaspoon of Lili Chutney over the top half of each roll. Spoon some of the nut chutney over the bottom half of each roll and top with some bhundi. Place a vada inside the roll and add a little Amli Chutney on top. Place a green chilli inside each vada pav and eat straight away.

ATHANU
SIDES, CHUTNEYS
& PICKLES

RAITA
COOLING YOGURT

Pickles add heat to a meal, whereas raita has the opposite effect; its purpose is to cool a spicy curry. Yogurt is always used in every raita recipe and this cooling combination of carrot, cucumber and green chilli works well together. Best of all, it's quick, easy and no cooking is required.

180 g/¾ cup plain yogurt
1 carrot, peeled and grated
¼ cucumber, grated
2 green chillies/chilis, chopped
1 teaspoon granulated sugar
½ teaspoon salt
1 teaspoon yellow mustard seeds

SERVES 2

Put the yogurt in a bowl and fold in the grated carrot and cucumber. Add the chopped chilli, sugar, salt and mustard seeds, then whisk to combine. Don't overwhisk otherwise the yogurt will split.

This yogurt can be stored in an airtight container in the fridge for up to 3 days.

TIP *If you are vegan, just replace the yogurt with a vegan alternative.*

MITHU DAHI
SWEET YOGURT

This sweetened yogurt brings coolness to a dish and balances the spiciness of other chutneys. This is ideal for street-food dishes, so make a batch of mithu dahi ahead of time, keep it in the fridge and then drizzle it over your food according to taste. Sometimes, I drizzle this sweet yogurt over a curry as an alternative to the cooling raita above.

125 ml/½ cup plain yogurt
⅛ teaspoon salt
1 tablespoon granulated sugar
pinch of ground ginger

SERVES 2

Put all the ingredients together in a bowl, then whisk to combine. Don't overwhisk otherwise the yogurt will split.

This yogurt can be stored in an airtight container in the fridge for up to 3 days.

TIP *If you are vegan, just replace the yogurt with a vegan alternative.*

SAMBHARO
SPICED SLAW
(V) (GF) (NF)

Sambharo is a Gujarati dish of grated cabbage and carrots stir-fried with a curry leaf *vagar* (tempered oil). I briefly stir-fry the vegetables until just slightly tender so that they retain their crunch and crispness. Sambharo is normally served as a side dish to a main meal, but I often serve it with Indian snacks such as Gathiya (see page 115). If I have leftover vegetables, I often make this and enjoy it as a simple salad.

½ small cabbage (about 200 g/ 7 oz.), cut into long thin strips
2 carrots, peeled and cut into 5-cm/2-in. matchsticks
4 teaspoons sunflower oil
½ teaspoon cumin seeds
⅓ teaspoon asafoetida
15 curry leaves
2 green chillies/chilis
½ teaspoon ground turmeric
½ teaspoon salt
½ teaspoon red chilli/chile powder
½ teaspoon fresh lemon juice

SERVES 4

Place the cabbage and carrots in a bowl and mix together.

Heat the oil in a frying pan/ skillet over a medium heat for 1 minute. Check if the oil is hot enough by dropping a few cumin seeds into the pan; if the seeds sizzle, the oil is ready.

Once the oil is hot enough, add the cumin seeds and stir gently for 20 seconds.

Add the asafoetida, curry leaves and green chillies to the oil and fry gently, stirring continuously, for 20 seconds to infuse the oil.

Add the cabbage and carrots, then stir to coat the veg in the spiced oil. Add the turmeric, salt and chilli powder and stir a few times, then add the lemon juice. Stir to mix all the ingredients together.

Once the stir-fried veg is tender but still firm, remove the pan from the heat and transfer the sambharo to a serving bowl.

If not serving straight away, this spiced slaw can be stored in an airtight container for up to 3 days in the fridge.

POSHO
GREEN BEAN & CARROTS COVERED IN MUSTARD SEEDS
(V) (GF) (NF)

This super-easy pickle can be made in minutes as no cooking is involved.
It has quite a bit of chilli heat in it and so is best served as a side dish
to milder curries.

1 small carrot, washed
50 g/1¾ oz. fine green beans,
  washed
5 green chillies/chilis
1 tablespoon yellow mustard
  seeds
⅛ teaspoon salt
⅛ teaspoon ground turmeric
1 tablespoon sunflower oil

SERVES 2

Peel the carrot and cut it into thin
matchsticks, about 5-cm/2-in long.
Top and tail the green beans.
    Place the carrot matchsticks
and green beans in a bowl and add
all the other ingredients. Mix well
to combine and then transfer to
a serving dish. Serve straight away.
    This pickled is best enjoyed
the day it is made.

TIPS *Adjust the amount of green
chilli in this dish to suit your taste.
This fresh pickle doesn't keep well,
so only make as much as you need.*

LAL CHUTNEY
ROASTED RED PEPPER & TOMATO CHUTNEY
(V) (GF) (NF)

This lal (meaning 'red' in Gujarati) chutney is used in street-food
dishes or as an accompaniment to bhajia (see pages 32–45).

1 red (bell) pepper, deseeded
  and chopped chunks
2 tomatoes, quartered
thumb-sized piece of fresh
  ginger, peeled and chopped
5 garlic cloves, peeled
2 tablespoons sunflower oil
½ teaspoon ground coriander
¼ teaspoon ground cumin
¼ teaspoon salt
½ teaspoon granulated sugar
3 tablespoons tomato ketchup
60 ml/¼ cup canned chopped
  tomatoes
2 green chillies/chilis
handful of fresh coriander/
  cilantro

SERVES 2

Preheat the oven to 160°C fan/
180°C/350°F/Gas 4.
    Place the red pepper and
tomatoes on a baking tray. Add the
ginger, garlic and sunflower oil and
mix to coat all the veg in the oil.
Roast in the hot oven for 20 minutes
until the peppers are soft and
tomatoes are starting to fall apart.
    Remove the tray from the oven
and leave to cool. Once everything
is cool enough to handle, remove
as much skin from the tomatoes
as possible.

Transfer the contents of the tray
to a food processor or blender and
add all the remaining ingredients.
Pulse until everything is roughly
combined but with some chunks.
Alternatively, you can blitz it to a
smooth consistency if preferred.
    This chutney can be stored in
an airtight container in the fridge
for up to 5 days.

*Pictured on the following page
with the Sweet Mango Chutney.*

BATAKU
SWEET MANGO CHUTNEY
(V) (GF) (NF)

Bataku is a Gujarati speciality and a great all-rounder. This green (unripe) mango chutney offers complex flavours and aromas, including the gentle warmth of cumin seeds. Serve this chutney alongside any curry or add it to a sandwich for some extra flavour.

60 ml/¼ cup sunflower oil
2 teaspoons cumin seeds
1 dried red chilli/chili
1 x 2-cm/1-in. long cinnamon
   stick, broken into small pieces
3 green cardamom pods
3 cloves
10 black peppercorns
⅓ teaspoon asafoetida
1 large green (unripe) mango,
   peeled and cut into 2–3-cm/
   1–1¼-in. pieces
200 g/1 cup granulated sugar

MASALA MIX
1 teaspoon red chilli/chile powder
½ teaspoon ground cinnamon
¼ teaspoon ground cardamom
¼ teaspoon salt

MAKES ABOUT 270 G/
1 GENEROUS CUP

Preheat the oven to 160°C fan/180°C/350°F/Gas 4.

Wash a heatproof glass jar and place it in the hot oven for 10–12 minutes to dry and sterilize. Carefully remove the jar from the oven and place it upside down on a clean dish towel to cool.

Heat the oil in a pan over a medium heat for 2–3 minutes and then add the cumin seeds. Once they start to crackle, add the dried red chilli, cinnamon stick, green cardamom pods, cloves, black peppercorns and asafoetida. Stir quickly and heat for 30 seconds.

Add the mango pieces and cook, stirring continuously, for 2 minutes; the mango will begin to dry out.

Reduce the heat to low and then stir in the sugar. Let the sugar dissolve and heat to a one-thread consistency. To check, dip a wooden spoon into the sugar syrup and let it cool as it will be very hot and could burn. Once cooled, touch the sugar syrup on the spoon with your forefinger, press your thumb and forefinger together and then gently pull them apart. One-thread consistency is when your forefinger and thumb are pulled apart, a single thread is formed and does not break.

Remove the pan from the heat and let the mango mixture cool for 10 minutes.

Add all the ingredients for the masala mix to the pan and gently stir to combine really well.

Transfer the chutney to the sterilized jar and store in a cool dry place for up to 2 weeks.

KERI NO CHUNDO
SWEET & SOUR GREEN MANGO PICKLE
(V) (GF) (NF)

Keri no chundo is a sticky, sweet and spicy mango pickle made using grated green (unripe) mango and spices. It's a delicious traditional relish that you will find in most Gujarati households. Try using a Rajapuri mango, if you can get hold of one, otherwise any green mango will do. Traditionally, keri no chundo is made by placing the mango mixture in a glass jar that is left in the hot sun so that the pickle cooks in a few days under the strong rays of the sun during the hot Indian summers. This is my cooked version, which is a must to take with us when we travel on a long journey or any road trips, and is perfect with theplas (see page 96).

1 large green (unripe) mango
60 ml/¼ cup sunflower oil
1 teaspoon cumin seeds
⅓ teaspoon asafoetida
2 dried red chillies/chilis
3 cloves
1 x 2-cm/1-in. long cinnamon stick
3 green cardamom pods
5 black peppercorns
250 g/1¼ cup granulated sugar

MASALA MIX
½ teaspoon ground cinnamon
¼ teaspoon salt
¼ teaspoon garam masala
½ teaspoon red chilli/chile powder
¼ teaspoon ground black pepper

SERVES 2–4

Preheat the oven to 160°C fan/180°C/350°F/Gas 4.

Wash a heatproof glass jar and place it in the hot oven for 10–12 minutes to dry and sterilize. Carefully remove the jar from the oven and place it upside down on a clean dish towel to cool.

Peel the mango, remove the stone/pit and grate/shred the flesh using the largest setting on a box grater.

Heat the oil in a pan over a medium heat for 2 minutes. Add the cumin seeds and when they start to crackle, add the asafoetida and dried chillies. Give the oil a quick stir and fry for 30 seconds. Add the cloves, cinnamon stick, cardamom pods and peppercorns.

Add the grated /shredded mango to the pan and cook, stirring continuously, for 2 minutes.

Reduce the heat to low and then stir in the sugar. Let the sugar dissolve and heat to a one-thread consistency. To check, dip a wooden spoon into the sugar syrup and let it cool as it will be very hot and could burn. Once cooled, touch the sugar syrup on the spoon with your forefinger, press your thumb and forefinger together and then gently pull them apart. One-thread consistency is when your forefinger and thumb are pulled apart, a single thread is formed and does not break.

Remove the pan from the heat and let the mango mixture cool for 4–5 minutes.

Add all the ingredients for the masala mix to the pan and gently stir to combine really well.

Transfer the pickle to the sterilized jar and store in cool dry place for up to 1 month.

AMLI CHUTNEY
DATE & TAMARIND CHUTNEY
(V) (GF) (NF)

A great all-round chutney – it's tangy, spicy and sweet and one of the most staple chutneys in Indian cooking.

100 g/3½ oz. dried tamarind block, broken into small pieces
480 ml/2 cups boiling water
100 g/⅔ cup dates, stoned/pitted and chopped into 2-cm/1-in. pieces
250 g/1¼ cups granulated sugar
250 g/9 oz. palm sugar/jaggery, grated
1 teaspoon salt
1 teaspoon red chilli/chile powder
2 tablespoons ground cumin
⅔ teaspoon black peppercorns, crushed to a powder in a pestle and mortar
2 teaspoons fennel seeds

MAKES 2 X 500-ML/17-OZ. JARS

Place the tamarind in a bowl, pour over half of the boiling water. Leave for 30 minutes.

Place the dates in a separate bowl and pour over the rest of the boiling water. Leave to soak for 30 minutes.

Sieve/strain the tamarind mixture into a third bowl to remove any seeds. If the mixture is too thick, add a splash of water to loosen.

Place the dates along with their soaking water in a blender and blitz to a smooth paste.

Place a large saucepan over a medium heat for 2–3 minutes. Add the tamarind and date mixtures to the pan along with all the remaining ingredients. Add 120 ml/½ cup water and cook, stirring continuously, for 25 minutes or until the chutney reduces and becomes quite thick. Keep stirring as the chutney cooks to make sure it doesn't burn.

Turn off the heat and let the chutney cool down in the pan, stirring occasionally. Once cooled, add enough cold water to achieve your preferred consistency.

Preheat the oven to 160°C fan/180°C/350°F/Gas 4 and sterilize two heatproof glasses (see page 143).

Transfer the chutney to the sterilized jars and store in fridge for up to 3 weeks.

LILI CHUTNEY
MINT, CORIANDER & CHILLI CHUTNEY
(V) (GF) (NF)

This super-fresh chutney instantly adds flavour and freshness to any meals or snacks it is served with. It also makes a great sandwich spread.

25 g/1 cup fresh mint leaves
50 g/2 cups fresh coriander/cilantro leaves
3 green chillies/chilis
thumb-sized piece of fresh ginger, peeled
5 garlic cloves, peeled
½ teaspoon salt
½ teaspoon cumin seeds
½ teaspoon fresh lemon juice
1 teaspoon granulated sugar

SERVES 1

Wash the fresh mint and coriander leaves in cold water and dry using kitchen paper.

Put all the ingredients in a food processor or blender and blitz until smooth.

Store in an airtight container in the fridge for up to 3 days.

LIMBU NU ATHANU

LEMON PICKLE

(V) (GF) (NF)

This is a lovely, fruity lemon pickle, which is very easy to make.
I have to admit, this one is my favourites! I always keep a jar or two
in my storecupboard. There's no cooking involved, just let the lemons
ferment in salt before adding the masala mix. The time it takes to
make this pickle will depend on the type of lemons you use. Try finding
lemons with a thin skin and be patient. The result is well worth it!

This pickle is delicious served with any curry, such as Chana Dal
(see page 78) or simply enjoy with breads, such as Tikka Thepla
(see page 96) or Aloo Paratha (see page 92).

500 g/1 lb. 2 oz. unwaxed lemons
2 tablespoons salt

MASALA MIX
300 g/1½ cups granulated sugar
1 teaspoon red chilli/chile powder
1 tablespoon ground coriander
1 tablespoon ground cumin
¼ teaspoon ground turmeric
1 tablespoon Kashmiri chilli/chile
powder

MAKES 2 X 500-ML/17-OZ. JARS

Thoroughly wash the lemons and
then cut them into chunks, roughly
1 cm/½ in. Place the lemon pieces
in a bowl, add the salt and mix
together. Cover the bowl and
place in a cool area for 7 days.

Each day, uncover the bowl
and shake the lemons to mix.
Repeat this for 7 days and then
check if the lemons are ready; the
lemons should break in between
your fingers. If they are not ready,
keep the bowl covered and
continue to shake every day.
Just be patient.

Once the lemons are
fermented, add all the ingredients
for the masala mix to the lemons
and mix very thoroughly.

Preheat the oven to 160°C fan/
180°C/350°F/Gas 4.

Wash two heatproof glass
jars and place in the hot oven for
10–12 minutes to dry and sterilize.
Carefully remove the jars from the
oven and place them upside down
on a clean dish towel to cool.

Transfer the pickle to the
sterilized jars and store in a cool
dark place for up to 6 months.

NOTE *This pickle can also be
added to curries when cooking
to add even more depth of flavour.*

MITHAI
SWEET THINGS

GAJAR HALWA
INDIAN CARROT PUDDING

Gajar Halwa is the most popular dessert served in our restaurant. 'Gajar' means 'carrots' in Gujarati, so this halwa is basically an Indian carrot pudding. The carrots are slow cooked in milk until all the liquid evaporates, which gives this pudding a wonderful flavour and a lovely soft texture. There are many ways to cook halwa; although my method is simple, it does take a little longer than others.

40 g/3 tablespoons ghee
2 large carrots, peeled and grated
60 ml/¼ cup full-fat/whole milk
75 g/⅓ cup granulated sugar
100 g/3½ oz. milk powder
1 teaspoon ground cardamom
2 teaspoons chopped toasted nuts (a mix of unsalted cashews, almonds and pistachios), plus extra to garnish
edible flowers, to garnish
coconut or vanilla ice cream, to serve

SERVES 4

Melt the ghee in a saucepan over a low flame. Add the grated carrot and stir for 3–4 minutes or until the carrots soften.

Add the milk to the pan and cook, stirring continuously, for 10–15 minutes or until the milk has evaporated and the carrots are nice and soft.

Add the sugar and continue stirring until it has dissolved into the carrot mixture. Make sure the mixture does not stick to the bottom of the pan.

Add the milk powder, and stir vigorously until it has completely combined with the carrots. Add the ground cardamom and chopped nuts, stir vigorously for 2–3 minutes, then take the pan off the heat.

Transfer the halwa to a plate garnish with a few chopped toasted nuts and edible flowers. Serve either cold or warm with a scoop of ice cream.

TIPS *Try using red carrots, if you can find them, otherwise normal carrots work just fine.*

We serve halwa in the restaurant with a very high-quality coconut gelato, however, it tastes just as delicious with vanilla ice cream or even on its own.

If you are planning on serving the halwa cold, you could transfer it to a mould or tray and leave to set, then unmould or cut into squares to serve.

KHEER
RICE PUDDING

This Indian rice pudding is simply lovely! It's a creamy dessert that is served at most festivals and celebrations in India. Kheer has always been one of our family's favourite comfort foods shared on cold winter evenings at home.

350 ml/scant 1½ cups full-fat/
  whole milk
50 ml/¼ cup condensed milk
50 g/1¾ oz. boiled rice (see page
  99 for method)
pinch of saffron
½ teaspoon ground cardamom
2 teaspoons chopped toasted
  nuts (a mix of unsalted cashews,
  almonds and pistachios)
2 tablespoons granulated sugar
pomegranate seeds and fresh
  mint leaves, to garnish

SERVES 4

Bring the milk to the boil in a heavy-based pan, then lower the heat and let the milk simmer for 2–3 minutes.

Add the condensed milk and gently cook for 3–4 minutes, stirring continuously to stop the mixture from burning on the bottom of the pan. The milk should now be a creamy consistency.

Add the cooked rice to the pan, stir gently, cover and continue simmering for 2–3 minutes.

Add the pinch of saffron and stir gently – saffron is very strong and so a little goes a long way.

Take the pan off the heat, add the cardamom, nuts and sugar. Continue stirring to ensure the sugar has dissolved completely and cardamom is evenly distributed.

Ladle the kheer into individual bowls and serve warm or cold, garnished with a few pomegranate seeds and mint leaves.

LAPSI
CRACKED WHEAT DESSERT

This is a traditional Indian sweet often eaten on religious occasions. There are two kinds of cracked wheat – coarse and fine. Always use the coarse variety here and be sure to cook the cracked wheat over a low heat to stop it burning.

2 tablespoons ghee
100 g/½ cup coarse cracked
  wheat
400 ml/1⅔ cups boiling water
50 g/1¾ oz. palm sugar/jaggery
pinch of saffron
1 teaspoon ground cardamom
2 teaspoons sultanas/golden
  raisins, plus extra to garnish
1 tablespoon chopped toasted
  nuts (a mix of unsalted cashews,
  almonds and pistachios)

SERVES 4

Melt the ghee in a saucepan over a low heat. Add the cracked wheat and cook, stirring, for 5 minutes or until it turns a rich brown colour.

Pour the boiling water into the pan with the browned wheat and stir until all the water has been absorbed by the wheat.

Add the palm sugar and, once it has melted, add the pinch of saffron, cardamom and sultanas. Continue stirring until all the sugar

has been absorbed and the lapsi mixture easily comes away from the sides of the pan.

Take the pan off the heat and leave the lapsi to cool slightly. Ladle into individual bowls and serve warm or cold, garnished with a few chopped nuts and sultanas

The lapsi can be stored in an airtight container in the fridge for up to 3 days.

LADOO

WHEAT FLOUR & PALM SUGAR SWEET

(NF)

Ladoos are considered to be a super food during the winter months in India as it is thought that the flour and palm sugar/jaggery keep the body warm.

150 g/1 cup plus 2 tablespoons
    wholemeal/whole-wheat flour
75 g/½ cup semolina
100 g/3½ oz. ghee (50 g/1¾ oz.
    melted, and 5 g/1¾ oz. set
    aside)
sunflower oil, for deep-frying
200 g/7 oz. grated palm sugar/
    jaggery
1 tablespoon ground cardamom
white poppy seeds, to decorate

MAKES 8 LADOOS

In a bowl, mix together the flour, semolina and melted ghee. Gradually add 90 ml/generous ⅓ cup water a little at a time, mixing until you have a soft, smooth dough. Divide the dough into pieces, each about 30 g/1 oz. in weight, and roll them into balls.

Place a heavy-based pan over a medium heat and add enough sunflower oil for deep-frying. Lower a few of the dough balls into the hot oil and fry for 3–4 minutes or until they turn golden brown. Remove the fried dough balls from the oil and place on kitchen paper to drain and cool. Repeat until all the dough balls have been fried

Break the fried dough balls into small pieces and blitz in a blender until the dough resembles fine breadcrumbs. Pass these crumbs through a sieve/strainer into a bowl. Return any crumbs too large to pass through the sieve to the blender and blitz again.

In a pan, melt the remaining ghee over a low heat. Add the grated palm sugar to the pan and mix thoroughly until the ghee and sugar are combined. Don't overcook this mixture as it will become solid and you'll have to start again.

Add the sugar-ghee mixture to the dough crumbs and stir gently. Add the cardamom and mix thoroughly. The resulting dough should now be moist.

Divide the moist dough into 8 equal-sized pieces. Use your hands to shape each piece into a dome. Transfer to a tray. Sprinkle the poppy seeds over the ladoos and leave to set firm.

These ladoos are best eaten when fresh, but they will keep for several days when stored in an airtight container.

TIP *Don't let the ladoo mixture cool down too much as it will become too hard to mould into shape; you need to work with it while it's still warm.*

SHEERO
SEMOLINA SWEET

This traditional Indian sweet is made from semolina. I make this at home often as it's quick to prepare and requires relatively few ingredients. I serve it at the end of a meal as it makes a lovely dessert. During Hindu festivals, sheero is offered to the gods as a blessing.

100 g/3½ oz. ghee
150 g/5½ oz. semolina
850 ml/3½ cups full-fat/whole milk
200 g/1 cup granulated sugar
1 teaspoon ground cardamom
2 teaspoons chopped toasted nuts (a mix of unsalted cashews, almonds and pistachios)
30 g/1 oz. sultanas/golden raisins (optional)

SERVES 6

Melt the ghee in a pan over a low heat. Add the semolina and fry until lightly golden, stirring continuously, to make sure it doesn't burn. The ghee will separate from the semolina around the edges of the pan.

Meanwhile, in a separate pan, bring the milk to the boil, then lower the heat and gently simmer.

Once the semolina is golden in colour, slowly and carefully add the milk to the pan – the mixture will spit once the milk is added, so do this over a sink.

Place the pan back on the heat, stirring continuously, until all the milk has been absorbed by the semolina. Within a few minutes the semolina will puff up and come away from the pan.

Add the sugar and continue stirring vigorously to make sure the mixture doesn't stick or burn. The sheero will weaken in consistency, but then the mixture will start to thicken in just a few minutes.

Add the cardamom and leave on the heat for a few more minutes, making sure the cardamom is distributed evenly. The sheero is ready once it comes away from the pan.

Remove the pan from the heat, stir the sheero and leave it to cool. Sprinkle the toasted nuts and sultanas, if using, on top. Enjoy warm or cold.

TIPS *It is important to keep stirring while you cook this dish; do not leave the pan unattended. Cook the sheero over a low to medium heat, but lower the heat if it's getting too hot. Also, make sure the milk has boiled before adding it to the semolina. Just be careful while adding the milk as the mixture will spit and sizzle.*

As with every recipe, sweetness is a personal preference. This dish can be very sweet, so adjust the amount of sugar according to your taste.

SHRIKHAND
SWEET STRAINED YOGURT

This is a hugely popular traditional dessert, served at weddings and festivals. It isn't difficult to make and doesn't require any cooking, however, you do need to allow quite a bit of time for the yogurt to drain. There are quicker recipes that use strained Greek yogurt, but this is the way I have always made it. Eat as a dessert or serve with Puri (see page 95) as part of a main meal.

500 g/2 cups plain yogurt
130 g/1 cup icing/confectioners' sugar
1 teaspoon ground cardamom
½ teaspoon full-fat/whole milk
large pinch of saffron
2 tablespoons chopped toasted nuts (a mix of unsalted cashews, almonds and pistachios)
pomegranate seeds and edible flowers, to garnish

muslin/cheesecloth

SERVES 4

Spoon the yogurt into the muslin, then gather and close the cloth at the top. Twist to expel any liquid. Keep on twisting, then tie a knot in the top of the cloth. Hang the cloth over a tap and leave for 12–15 hours to let the whey drain out of the yogurt.

Remove the cloth from the tap and place the drained yogurt in a bowl. Add the sugar and cardamom and whisk to a smooth texture.

Place a sieve/strainer over a bowl and then press the yogurt through the sieve.

In a small bowl, combine the milk and saffron and mix gently. Place the bowl in a microwave and heat for 10 seconds on a high setting. Add this saffron milk to the yogurt.

Gently fold 1 tablespoon of the nuts into the shrikhand, which should still have a rich, creamy texture. Cover the bowl with cling film/plastic wrap and chill the shrikhand in the fridge for a few hours.

Spoon the shrikhand into individual bowls and garnish with the remaining nuts, pomegranate seeds and edible flowers. The shrikhand can be stored in the fridge for up to 1 week.

TIPS *You want nice, thick consistency, so don't whisk the shrikhand too vigorously as it will end up too runny. Always fold the ingredients into the strained yogurt.*

If you don't have any saffron, you can just add a few drops of yellow food colouring instead.

PINUM
DRINKS

MASALA CHAI
SPICED TEA
(GF) (NF)

Indians love chai! Masala chai is made by simmering tea leaves with aromatic spices, which is then boiled with milk. The result is a lovely warm, fragrant brew. There is no right or wrong here; simply adjust the ratio of masala chai spice blend, sugar and milk to suit your taste.

½ teaspoon Masala Chai Spice
  Blend (see below)
1 teabag or 1 teaspoon loose-leaf
  tea
1 teaspoon granulated sugar
120 ml/½ cup full-fat/whole milk

SERVES 1

Bring 240 ml/1 cup water to the boil in a pan over a high heat. Lower the heat, add the masala chai spice blend and the teabag or loose-leaf tea and leave it to brew for 1 minute.

Add the sugar and milk to the pan, raise the heat to high and bring to the boil again. Reduce the heat and leave it the masala chai to simmer for a couple of minutes.

Strain the chai into heatproof glasses and serve straight away.

NOTE *Although this recipe makes one drink, it can easily be doubled or tripled to serve more.*

MASALA CHAI SPICE BLEND
(V) (GF) (NF)

This is a wonderfully fragrant masala chai spice blend that will take your tea to the next level. Every family has their own spice blend and this is mine.

3 tablespoons whole green
  cardamom
2 tablespoons black peppercorns
2 tablespoons cloves
15-cm/6-in. long cinnamon stick,
  broken into pieces
3 tablespoons fennel seeds
1 tablespoon whole black
  cardamom
1 whole nutmeg, crushed in
  a pestle and mortar
4 tablespoons ground ginger

MAKES ABOUT 125 G/4½ OZ.
(ENOUGH FOR ABOUT 45 CUPS
OF MASALA CHAI)

Place a frying pan/skillet over a low heat and add the green cardamom, black peppercorns, cloves, cinnamon stick, fennel seeds and black cardamom. Lightly toast for 4–5 minutes, moving the spices continuously to make sure they don't catch on the heat.

Remove the spices from the pan, spread over a plate and let cool.

Transfer the spices to a blender, add the crushed nutmeg and blitz to a fine powder.

Remove from the blender, add the ground ginger and mix well.

The spice blend can be stored in an airtight container for up to 6 months for you to use whenever you fancy a cup of masala chai.

MITHI LASSI
SWEET YOGURT DRINK
GF NF

Lassis comes in three main varieties: sweet, salty and mango.
They pair well with spicy food as the yogurt naturally cools
the taste buds. Our sweet lassi is a rich, decadent drink, simple
to make and hugely popular in the restaurant.

240 ml/1 cup full-fat (5%) plain
  yogurt
2 tablespoons vanilla ice cream
1½ tablespoons icing/
  confectioners' sugar
100 ml/generous ⅓ cup full-fat/
  whole milk
a few ice cubes (optional)

TO GARNISH
pinch of ground cumin
a few pomegranate seeds

SERVES 1

Place the yogurt, ice cream and
sugar in a bowl and gently mix
with a spatula to combine.
　　Add the milk to the bowl and
use a handheld blender to blitz the
mixture until smooth.
　　Fill a tall glass with a few ice
cubes, if using, and then pour over
the lassi. Garnish the drink with a
pinch of cumin and some
pomegranate seeds. Serve straight
away. If the lassi is quite thick, serve
with a spoon.

CHAAS
SPICED YOGURT DRINK
GF NF

Traditional chaas is made by blending cold yogurt with water
and any spices you like, but I like mine simply with salt and cumin.
This is a lovely refreshing drink served alongside main meals or
enjoyed on its own on hot summer days.

260 ml/generous 1 cup plain
  yogurt
½ teaspoon salt
¼ teaspoon ground cumin
a few ice cubes
pinch of toasted cumin seeds,
  to garnish

SERVES 2

Combine the yogurt, salt and
ground cumin in a bowl with
160 ml/⅔ cup water and whisk
to combine well. When the chaas
foams, the drink is ready to serve.
　　Fill two tall glasses with a few
ice cubes and then pour over the
chaas. Garnish the drinks with a
few toasted cumin seeds. Serve
straight away.

MANGO LASSI
MANGO YOGURT DRINK
(GF) (NF)

Lassis come in all kinds of flavours but mango is probably the most popular. Mangoes grow abundantly in India but it is not always easy to find flavourful ripe mangoes elsewhere, so I often use canned mango pulp instead. This lassi is basically like a fruit smoothie, which is great for breakfast or dessert.

220 g/scant 1 cup plain yogurt
480 ml/1¾ cups canned mango
    pulp
1 tablespoon icing/confectioners'
    sugar
a few ice cubes (optional)

TO GARNISH
diced fresh mango
pomegranate seeds
fresh mint sprigs

SERVES 2

Place the yogurt, mango pulp and icing sugar in a blender and blitz until combined well.

Fill two tall glasses with a few ice cubes, if using, and then pour over the lassi. Garnish the drinks with a few pieces of fresh mango, some pomegranate seeds and a sprig of mint. Serve straight away.

TIPS *I like my mango lassi quite thick, but you can adjust the amount of yogurt according to your preference.*

If you can find it, try using mango pulp made from Kesar or Alphonso mangoes. Otherwise, don't worry too much about the variety.

LIMBU NU PANI
HOMEMADE LEMONADE
(V) (GF) (NF)

Limbu means 'lemon' in Gujarati and *pani* means 'water'. This super-refreshing homemade lemonade is ideal to serve on a hot day. Summers in Gujarat are very hot and it is thought that limbu nu pani helps to fight against heatstroke and rehydrates the body.

1 lemon
½ teaspoon salt
3 tablespoons granulated sugar
¼ teaspoon cumin seeds, crushed
    in a pestle and mortar

TO GARNISH
lemons wedges
1 teaspoon salt
a few ice cubes
handful of fresh mint leaves
    (optional)

SERVES 2

Fill a bowl with 280 ml/1 generous cup water and squeeze in the juice of the lemon. Add the salt, sugar and cumin seeds and stir to combine.

Rub a lemon wedge around the rims of two tall glasses. Spread the salt over a shallow saucer. Turn each glass upside down and slowly dip the rim in the salt. Go gently and stop once there is a fine layer of salt around the rim of the glass.

Fill each glass with a handful of ice cubes, lemon wedges and mint leaves, if using, then pour over the lemonade. Serve straight away.

THANDAI
COLD MILK WITH NUTS & SEEDS

Thandai is a refreshing milk drink that is popular during the Holi festival season. The term 'thandai' is derived from the word *thanda* in Gujarati meaning 'cool' and this drink is made using nuts and spices, which are said to have a cooling effect on the body. The beauty of this recipe is that the spice mix can be made ahead and stored, so whenever I want thandai, I simply blitz all the other ingredients together with a couple of tablespoons of the spice mix. You can easily adjust the quantity of spice mix and sugar in this recipe to suit your taste.

240 ml/1 cup full-fat/whole milk
1 tablespoon granulated sugar
2 tablespoons Thandai spice mix
   (see below)
2 tablespoons vanilla ice cream
a few ice cubes (optional)
pinch of edible dried rose petals,
   to garnish

SERVES 1

To make *Thandai*, place the milk, sugar, thandai spice mix and ice cream in a food processor or blender and blitz to the consistency of a milkshake.

Fill a tall glass with a few ice cubes, if using, and then pour over the thandai. Garnish the drink with a few edible dried rose petals. Serve straightaway.

THANDAI SPICE MIX
Ⓥ ⒼⒻ

1¼ tablespoons unsalted almonds
1¼ tablespoons unsalted
   cashews
1¼ tablespoons unsalted
   pistachios
1¼ tablespoons fennel seeds
pinch of freshly ground black
   pepper
2 teaspoons melon seeds
1¼ tablespoons white poppy
   seeds
2 teaspoons cardamom seeds
large pinch of saffron
½ teaspoon freshly grated
   nutmeg
½ teaspoon ground ginger

MAKES ABOUT 125 G/4½ OZ.
(ENOUGH FOR ABOUT 4 CUPS
OF THANDAI)

To make the spice mix, place a frying pan/skillet over a medium heat for 2–3 minutes. Turn off the heat and add the almonds, cashews and pistachios to the pan. Gently shake the pan. After 30 seconds, add all the remaining ingredients for the spice mix to the pan and gently stir for 3 minutes.

Transfer the spice mix to a grinder and blitz to a fine powder. Once the spice mix is completely cool, it can be stored in an airtight container until needed.

INDEX

ACKNOWLEDGEMENTS

It is fair to say, writing does not come naturally; I am much more comfortable in the kitchen. The process can be compared to a trip to India – incredibly difficult, but always incredibly moving! After cooking for over 72 years, writing this book has taken me hugely out of my comfort zone, however, I am so proud of *Manju's Cookbook*.

It is with huge thanks to my publishers Ryland Peters and Small – especially Megan, Leslie, Abi and Julia. Thank you for all your hard work in making this book beautiful. I know it hasn't been easy. We have faced obstacles along our journey together and I really appreciate your patience, love and guidance.

Thank you, Hannah, for sourcing all the gorgeous props for the photo shoots.

I have said many times that I am truly blessed! I have the love and support of the most amazing family. Thank you to my two sons, Jaymin and Naimesh! They made my dream come true by gifting Manju's, our much-loved restaurant, to me on my 80th birthday. A huge thank you to my two daughter-in-laws, Dee and Kirti, who work alongside me in the kitchen. My family have made Manju's what it is today. It's been an incredible ride together but I have no plans to hang up my apron yet!

A huge thank you to my younger brother, Vinod. He had the belief in me since we were little and he would always encourage me to open a restaurant. Well, it took a while, but it did happen!

To Troy Willis, your food styling is exceptional, I loved watching you work during our photoshoots together.

Clare Winfield – you are truly a wonderful human being and we are blessed to have you as a dear friend. You worked your magic! The photos are stunning and we couldn't be more happy. It is because of your love and friendship that this book has come about. Thank you for bringing RPS and us together.

It is to my late husband that I thank the most! You passed away while this book was being written. You were my biggest supporter! I would show you photos of the food taken by Clare and you would give me the biggest smile. Well, I know you are smiling down on me from above! I love you and miss you every day.

Lastly, to my dear readers, thank you for buying my book. I hope you have fun cooking my recipes and sharing them with your friends and family. I hope you gain a better understanding about vegetarian Indian food, especially the wonderful cuisine of Gujarat.